A More Brilliant Life

"Jake and Kylie have crafted something remarkable—a memoir that reads like a trusted friend sharing their most transformative journey. Their vulnerability in portraying midlife upheaval on a Minnesota farm, then courageously rebuilding in Costa Rica, creates space for readers to see their own possibilities more clearly. They seamlessly weave raw personal narrative with actionable insights and thoughtful recommendations. As someone who has also rebuilt life internationally, I deeply admire their generosity in mapping this territory for others."

—Olga Brouwer, M.B.A., A.C.C., Life & Leadership Coach,
Former Executive Director Minnesota Agriculture & Rural Leadership (MARL)

"*A More Brilliant Life* is an incredible book with simple but deeply impactful tools that will ACTUALLY change your life. Kylie and Jake prove that you can create a life of deep alignment and profound joy by taking meaningful small steps each day. They show you that it doesn't have to be overwhelming to change your life. This book has something for everyone, no matter where you are on your journey. It has been an honor to be a part of and to witness their commitment to living a life they love and can be proud of. Kylie and Jake are inspiring, down to earth REAL people who will lovingly take your hand and guide you to your most brilliant life."

—Tacy Nielson, Spiritual Life Coach,
Energy Medicine Practitioner and International Retreat Host

"I absolutely love this book. Beautifully written, full of wisdom."

—Dan Simon, Simon Mediation, Transformative Mediator, Trainer,
Co-Author of *Self Determination in Mediation*

"*A More Brilliant Life* is an inspiring and transformative guide to reclaiming your health, purpose, and direction. Kylie and Jake have done a phenomenal job walking readers through the process of personal growth, offering thoughtful, empowering advice and practical tools to help you take ownership of your path. Their story will resonate with anyone seeking to live with intention—and proves that change is not only possible, but powerful. Whether you're searching for your 'why' or ready to level up in life, this book will move and motivate you."

—Jeff and Brandy Toomer, Co-owners of New Ulm Fitness,
Personal Trainers, Competitive Athletes

Praise for *A More Brilliant Life*

"Honest, accessible, and relatable—Kylie and Jake's story shows that it's not only possible to make a huge life change when we're languishing...it's imperative to our health and happiness. They offer pearls of wisdom far beyond their years. This book is for anyone searching for the courage to choose joy, and who is willing to take an introspective look at their own life."

—Brie Taralson, Fellow Joy-seeker, Owner of Lykke Books bookstore,
Founder of Ulm Sweet Ulm community hub

"A More Brilliant Life is the kind of book that meets you where you are, whether you're feeling stuck, going through a transition, or simply longing for more meaning and joy in your everyday life. With honesty, insight, and soul-nourishing guidance, Kylie and Jake offer practical tools that help you remember who you are at your core, realign with what truly matters, and begin building a life that feels deeply fulfilling. A beautiful and inspiring read that I'll be recommending often!"

—Rachel Vorwerk, HHP, MBSR-P,
Holistic Health and Energy Medicine Practitioner

"Kylie and Jake's brilliant life journey is simultaneously relatable and inspirational. They incorporate their experiences, the highs and the lows, into actionable steps that anyone can take to construct their own brilliant life."

—Chris DT Gordon, M. Ed., Professional Speaker,
Author of *From Survivor to Striver*

"A More Brilliant Life is a raw, honest, and empowering guide for anyone ready to break free from the life they've outgrown. Kylie and Jake's vulnerability is both relatable and inspiring—and their journey offers practical tools for rediscovering joy, purpose, and possibility. I found myself nodding, tearing up, and feeling genuinely hopeful. This book is a gift for anyone navigating a midlife reset."

—Gwen Russell, Founder of Spark Health Coaching
and C.O.R.E. Bungee Fitness

Rise
Above Expectations
Discover
Who You Are
Reclaim
Your Future

A More
Brilliant
Life

Kylie Rieke with Jake Rieke

PRESS

A More Brilliant Life: Rise Above Expectations. Discover Who You Are. Reclaim Your Future.

Copyright © 2025 Kylie Rieke with Jake Rieke

Published by StoryBuilders Press

eBook: 979-8-89833-000-2

Paperback: 979-8-89833-001-9

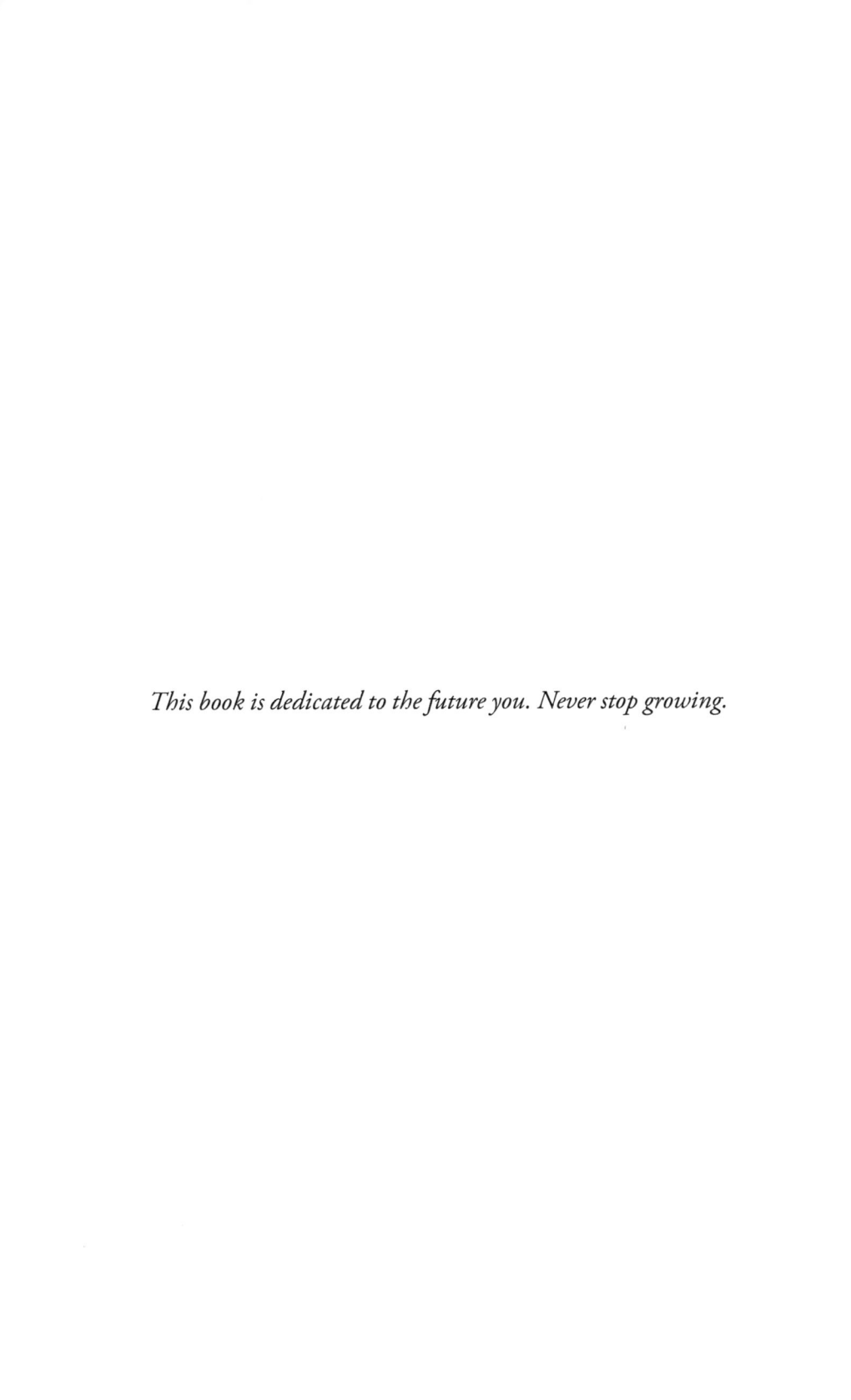

This book is dedicated to the future you. Never stop growing.

Contents

Foreword

There are moments in life when you encounter people whose journey changes your own—and for me, Kylie and Jacob are exactly those people.

From the first time I heard their story, I was struck by their courage. They weren't just surviving the weight of expectations, inherited roles, and societal norms—they were dismantling them with raw honesty and rebuilding a life with intention, alignment, and purpose. *A More Brilliant Life* is not just a book; it is a brave testament to transformation.

This book doesn't offer quick fixes or polished clichés. Instead, it invites you into the real, messy, courageous unraveling of two people who chose to let go of a life that looked good on the outside to build one that felt good on the inside. Kylie and Jacob take you by the hand through breakdowns, breakthroughs, identity crises, and soul awakenings. And they do it with compassion, clarity, and a deep desire to help others do the same.

I had the great honor of walking alongside them for part of this journey—witnessing the questions, the discomfort, the lightbulb moments, and the small wins that turned into lasting shifts. I didn't just watch them change their lives. I saw them reclaim their power, and in doing so, give others permission to do the same.

To know Kylie and Jacob is to know integrity, curiosity, and grit. I'm proud to call them not only collaborators in growth—but lifelong friends. And I believe that by the end of this book, you'll feel the same way.

So, wherever you are right now—stuck, searching, or simply sensing there's more—I hope you read this book not just with your eyes, but with your heart wide open. It might just be the beginning of your own more brilliant life.

With admiration and gratitude,
Dr. Julie Wilkes, Ph.D. Org Psychology
Author, TEDx Motivational Speaker, Podcaster, Certified Business and Executive Coach

CHAPTER 1

Rock Bottom

I couldn't make myself get out of bed. I didn't even have the energy to turn my head when my husband and two-year-old daughter walked cautiously into the bedroom.

The only words I managed to speak were, "I feel so . . . unimportant." And the truth of that statement sank deep into my soul.

Yesterday was my thirtieth birthday.

My husband, Jake, spent the entire day working—too busy to come home for a single moment. He was gone when I woke up that morning and still gone when I went to bed. I spent the evening eating half of my birthday cake right out of the container and went to bed. Alone.

Work always came first. I had accepted that for the other 364 days of the year. In fact, I had also accepted it on my other birthdays, the ones that did not end with a 0. But this one was supposed to celebrate a new decade of my life. And the reason he didn't have time? He had to "pick rocks." It was a tedious, never-ending farm task of driving through fields and removing stones that had surfaced. He was a farmer, and the farm was more important than all of us, no matter what day it was. So, we had actually fallen *below rock bottom*, because the rocks were more important than us, too.

What happened?!

Our lives now only revolved around work, chores, errands, and responsibilities. Our few moments of reprieve were spent numbing the pain with screens, junk food, alcohol, and shopping for things that we never had time to enjoy. We had become zombies trudging around in a life that we thought we had to live. We were depressed, overweight, unhealthy, and lethargic. We hated the people we had become. We felt stuck in our existence, and could not imagine any way to ever free ourselves from it.

Is this what being an adult is supposed to be like?

On the outside, we had it all. A big house and a nice car. A loving family with a toddler and another one on the way. We were running the family business, proving our loyalty and worth with a strong bottom line. All our needs were being taken care of including the scariest of all—health insurance. But at what cost? Inside we were slowly dying.

I wish I could say that hitting *below rock bottom* was a turning point in our lives. I wish I could say that I stood up for myself confidently and eloquently. I wish I could say we both realized the insanity of our situation.

But we were stuck.

We were so deeply entrenched in the wrong life that it took about a decade to slowly apply the brakes, start moving in the right direction, and find our true selves again. In a sense, my thirtieth birthday was the perfect foreshadowing of the difficult decade ahead.

It was a challenging, painful, and exhilarating journey out of darkness. To crawl our way out, it took a midlife crisis, a midlife awakening, a trip to the emergency room, a marathon, countless books, apps, and podcasts, experimenting with every personal development method and health strategy we could find, and pushing ourselves to the limits. Each small step forward opened our world to more possibilities. Each small habit change made us feel lighter, and the future brighter. We reclaimed hope and joy in our lives again.

By my fortieth birthday, I was empowered and confident. I planned and celebrated in a way that was meaningful to me, and Jake chose to spend the entire weekend with me over one of the most important farm duties there is—planting. (For those of you who aren't familiar with farming in the Midwest, planting is *untouchable*.)

This is the story of how two farm kids from rural Minnesota slowly woke up in a middle-aged nightmare, woke up to see the forces that sucked us into that nightmare, what we did to unwind everything we had put into motion, and how we are creating a new life, a new identity, and continuously discovering the path to living in alignment with our inner beings.

We got ourselves out of an impossible situation and we want to share everything we learned. We know how painful it is to completely lose yourself. We know how overwhelming it feels to question the life you are supposed to live. But it is never too late; it is never too complicated.

It's okay to admit that you aren't happy. It's okay to admit that your life isn't what you want it to be. It's okay if you want to change. It's okay, it's possible, and you absolutely can.

Our Self-Inflicted Limits

Like many people, we were so stuck that for a long time, we couldn't even see we were stuck. It felt like the world was dragging us around, and life was all based on luck and circumstance.

We allowed the expectations that we perceived from others to dictate our entire lives, everything from beliefs, values, work ethic, daily schedule, likes and dislikes. And we were doing a damn good job at it. We looked successful. We had the American dream.

The problem was that it wasn't *our* dream. Deep inside, our souls were miserable.

We thought this was normal.

We started using unhealthy coping mechanisms to numb the pain. The more we ate and drank, the heavier we got. The more we shopped, the heavier our house got. The more we glued ourselves to screens, the more our brains tuned out. We thought these coping mechanisms were helping us, but in reality, they were keeping us trapped even more. We were in a heavy daze.

It took some very painful experiences below rock bottom for us to start questioning our lives. What we eventually found was that nothing was *physically* keeping us stuck. The imaginary chains were limiting beliefs inside our own minds. They created fears about the world, doubts about our capabilities, and blinded us from all the possibilities.

It is scary how extensive and how ingrained our limiting beliefs can be, and we had a LOT of them:

* Your job is more important than you.
* Life is supposed to be a struggle.

* Doing what you love to do is considered a hobby, never a career.
* There is never enough money.
* Once you become an adult, your life is decided.
* Once you have kids, you can no longer focus on yourself.
* You must work hard until you retire. Then you can relax and go on vacation.
* The older you get, the more unhealthy you get, and there is nothing you can do about it.
* Once you agree to take over a family business, it is a life-long sentence.

Our limiting beliefs created unhealthy habits. Our unhealthy habits drained our energy and confidence and made it impossible to question our limiting beliefs. It was a self-perpetuating cycle downward.

How Did We Get So Lost?

When you were a kid, do you remember feeling like the possibilities were limitless and the world was magical? Children are naturals at knowing who they are and listening to their intuition. They can tell you their favorite games, hobbies, foods, and colors. They don't care what other people think.

Sadly, we allow society to slowly drain our dreams and fill our heads with limiting beliefs instead. As I grew up, I was told repeatedly that art was a hobby, but not a profession. (Unless I became an art teacher, in which case, that would be a legitimate career.) Jake wanted to be an astronaut. I wanted to live on every continent. Jake wanted to be a psychologist. I wanted to be an actor on Broadway. Jake wanted to play the drums. I wanted to bike across the country from east to west. Jake wanted to canoe across the country from north to south.

After enough time, we were persuaded to agree that none of these dreams were realistic and to settle down with a sensible job that paid the bills. So, after serving two years in the United States Peace Corps, (which was a sensible way to get adventure out of our systems) we returned to Minnesota and agreed to take the role of Farmer and Farmer's Wife. But if you rely on the identity of a job or a responsibility, then that identity is going to absorb you. And it did.

By the time we were in our thirties, Jake could not even answer the question, "What do you like to do?"

The scariest part is realizing how many people are in this exact same nightmare. People completely forget who they are and what their purpose is. They hide away their unique passions and skills. They restrain their curiosity and playfulness. They resort to habits and addictions that provide short-term relief but have long-term consequences. They become weighed down physically, mentally, and emotionally.

Seeing the Signs

So how did we finally wake up? There was not a monumental *Ah-hah* moment that stopped us in our tracks. There were no clouds that miraculously parted. Although this may be true for some people, we needed a lot of wake-up calls before we finally opened our eyes. Looking back at our journey, there were many moments and many signs that changed the course of our lives. Some were obvious, others were resisted, and some were missed completely. But in hindsight, they were everywhere.

Some signs were scary, like being diagnosed with pre-diabetes. When the test results came back, I was shocked and embarrassed. I didn't want anyone to know, but it was the wake-up call I needed for my diet. I began looking at nutrition labels, realized the crazy amount of sugar I was consuming, and started eating healthier.

Some signs were depressing. Jake was pictured on the cover of *Progressive Farmer* magazine. It should have been a proud moment. Sadly, he was at the heaviest weight of his entire life and the framed picture was hidden away. He decided he did not want to stay in the obese weight category, and started cutting back on calories.

Some signs were emotional. Jake traveled to Cambodia with a leadership program and it resurfaced all his memories from our days in the Peace Corps. We had served two years in rural El Salvador, living without modern luxuries, and also without modern stress, depression, and expectations. It was a massive wake-up call when he compared it to our current life. We wanted that freedom back.

Some signs were frustrating. We tried to work out a business plan to transition and purchase the family farm from the previous generation, but we hit roadblock after roadblock. No matter how much time and energy we invested, it wasn't meant to be. We had to learn how to let go.

Some signs were spiritual. When my dad passed away in 2010, my sister told me that an eagle was his sign to us. I brushed it off and didn't believe her. But after many years, I have finally accepted that she was right. Whenever I see an eagle, I feel his love and support.

Some signs were abrupt, like our kids wanting to change schools in the middle of a school year. It was in a nearby town where we would later move. (And guess what the new school mascot was? An eagle, of course.) Luckily we allowed our kids to guide us.

Some signs slowly grew over time until they were too much to bear, and we could no longer ignore them. Our weight. Our possessions. Our stress. Our depression.

Some signs were the words coming out of our own mouths. But we weren't listening to ourselves or taking it seriously. I was once talking with a friend about planning to move to a warmer climate. To my surprise, she wasn't surprised at all. Apparently, I had told her this desire many times. She had been listening closer to me than I was.

All the signs will steer you in the right direction if you can start paying attention to them. We had to quiet our minds and be willing to listen. We had to accept that we weren't actually happy. We had to realize that there were underlying causes of our unhealthy addictions. We had to be courageous to do things that other people thought were completely crazy.

You have probably noticed some of the signs in your own life:

* Do you eat in response to your feelings, instead of your hunger?
* Do you drink alcohol to forget your problems?
* Do you always keep yourself uber busy and distracted?
* Is there something you wish you had time to do, but can't get past your daily to-do list?
* Is there something that you make your kids do or that you urge your friends to do, but aren't doing yourself?
* Are you listening to the jokes or sarcastic comments coming out of your own mouth?
* Do you have regrets that you can't seem to shake?

* Is depression or anxiety your normal baseline emotion?
* Do you suppress your feelings, or do you experience a lot of highs or lows?
* Are there recurring coincidences, themes, symbols, information, or people that show up at just the right moment?

It's time to start tuning into the signs around you and within you. The signs are everywhere, but you have to stop, listen, accept, and follow them.

The Path Forward

We started changing our lives in very slow increments. Tiny habit changes that started adding up fast. We had a long way to go in almost every category you can think of. But when you start replacing habits that make you feel bad with habits that make you feel good, it's a game changer. It is exciting and empowering. You gain confidence which helps you continue. Everything gets easier when you feel better, and when you are doing it for the right reasons.

We started eliminating our unhealthy coping mechanisms one by one. The first and most significant transformation was how clear our minds became. When our haze lifted, we looked around at our situation in disbelief. We could not believe what we had been putting up with. We could not believe how we had been treating ourselves and how we were letting other people treat us.

Clearing the fog can be painful at first because you will have to face all the things you were trying to avoid in the first place. And some may have grown into monsters. But with your newfound superpowers, you will be able to take on the challenge.

Be careful: If you don't face those monsters, the coping mechanisms will come right back. Or you will replace them with others.

We found ways to find those deeper issues and confront them. It felt impossible and daunting at first. One step at a time, we were able to chip away at the chains we had put around ourselves. With commitment and persistence, we gained massive momentum. We challenged our limiting beliefs and current situation. We resigned from our jobs. We moved our family from a spacious farmsite with a big house to a two-bedroom/one-bath apartment. We had to let go of a lot of things, including my pottery studio, our vehicles, pontoon, RV, and the majority of our possessions. But now we have time to spend with each other instead of working all day, every day. Life has become a beautiful journey instead of a slow, stiff, heavy shuffle toward the grave.

This book is intended to share with you everything we did to break the chains of our old life. We tried everything that came our way. We read, listened, watched, experimented, and learned as much as possible. Some ideas will resonate with you, others won't. You don't have to try everything, but please have an open mind and experiment with the ones that intrigue you. The most important step is to simply *take a step* and try something new.

The Brilliant Life Journey is an action plan that condenses everything we learned into six phases: Contemplate, Investigate, Activate, Eliminate, Accelerate, and Navigate. It's a process to help guide you down your own path. There are a variety of areas and action steps within each phase, so you can pick and choose what is right for you. They can be done in any order, and you might circle back or rotate between a few of them. In the end, they all build on each other and each one spirals your life up to the next level.

We will dedicate a chapter to each of the phases in The Brilliant Life Journey and go into detail about all the amazing ways to implement them into your life. Feel free to jump around the chapters and read the one that you need at the moment. Just know that they are all connected— just like our minds, bodies, and emotions. Each area builds off the strength of the others. You can weave in any direction and design that you need to, but make sure you include them all.

Here is a quick preview of The Brilliant Life Journey's six phases:

Contemplate: Silence the unnecessary external noise and slow down. Understand yourself and assess your life. Then take a step back for a broader perspective.

Investigate: Get curious and learn as much as possible. Create your own motivation. Experiment with new things and reignite the old. Challenge and question everything.

Activate: Start habits, routines, and activities that level up your physical, mental, emotional, and spiritual health. Take back control and lean into love.

Eliminate: Get rid of unhealthy behavior patterns, thought patterns, and anything harming you or preventing your growth. Then, start crafting a new you with an intentionally lighter life.

Accelerate: Build momentum and take everything to the next level: your health, your community, and your mindset. Start seeing possibilities and realizing your dreams.

Navigate: Guide your relationships toward a brighter future. Take ownership of what you contribute, and support others in an empowering way. Align your lives, grow together, and unite with integrity.

Begin Again

There is a reason we feel stuck. It is a way for our feelings to communicate with us when we don't stop and listen to our intuition, and when we don't do the things that really matter. If you are feeling stuck in any area of your life, let's find out what's causing it. Then take some responsibility and action steps to change it. It's probably something really, really important that you are doing a great job of avoiding. We went through so much in the past decade that we want to share with you. You don't have to spend a decade like we did; we want you to use these techniques and information so you can reach new levels of your own life as quickly as possible. And if it can help you in any way, then writing this book was worth it.

The most exciting part is that there is no end to the journey. There is no end to the joy you can find. There is no maximum amount of personal development. The journey continues to unfold for us, and we are always finding deeper levels within ourselves. We constantly try new things and question the old. We sometimes forget and have to relearn. We lean into the habits and choices that bring us value, and let go of what no longer serves us. It is a perpetual cycle through these action steps.

Jake and I always knew there was more to life than our current situation, but we never felt that we deserved it. The journey that we went on has revealed to us that we do deserve it. We all deserve it.

We first had to empower ourselves by elevating our physical, mental, emotional, and spiritual health. After we were able to start seeing ourselves differently, we gained confidence that we were worthy of the life that we wanted. We started taking responsibility and action toward it, and no longer played the victim. This is what we want for you. You can move through this life with more ease and more confidence. You can be present and joyful. You can find the *you* that is hidden deep inside. **You can take control of your life and change it.**

The world is simply a mirror reflecting back what you think of yourself. So your journey must start with you. Change the way you see yourself, and the world will change the way it sees you.

CHAPTER 2

The Progression of Our Pain

E ven before we left the house, I ignored the warning signs.

"I don't think that road has been plowed," Jake said with hesitation and confusion.

It was winter in Minnesota, but the cold temperature and a couple feet of snow weren't going to stop me. I was determined to go for a hike at a nearby state park. We were in desperate need of exercise and fresh air. We had bundled up for the weather and were ready to battle the elements.

The tiny, winding gravel road was the back entrance to the state park. It was much closer than the main entrance and would save us time. As usual, I was trying to maximize our schedule, and we had to pick up our kids from the bus stop in an hour.

We turned off the highway and onto the treacherous path. Jake protested from the passenger's seat, "What are we doing?! We can't drive on this road!" He was wide-eyed and peering nervously over the hood of the car while gripping the armrests. Jake knew the risk of driving on a layer of hard-packed snow which could give way at any moment, and we would sink straight down into the soft snow below.

"We'll be fine," I brushed him off. "We don't have time to drive around to the other entrance."

I drove over the giant snow drifts, just guessing where the road was. But it didn't concern me at all. We didn't have time to be concerned. If we just kept moving forward and stuck to the plan, everything would be fine. We would park the car, walk around the brisk trails, and feel so much better afterward. I couldn't see or hear any of the red flags, including my husband.

I was completely unaware.

Until the car slowly started sliding to the left.

I wasn't going fast, so I easily stopped the car. *No problem.* We were just slipping off the road that I couldn't actually see. All I needed to do was reverse the car and get back on the invisible road. I started backing up, but the car slipped more to the left as it went backward. *Okay, no problem.* I put the car back in drive, cranked the steering wheel to the right, and stepped on the gas. But instead of going right, the car pulled even more to the left, and with a final thud, it sank deep into the snow. The car was sitting at a very unsettling angle, just like my stomach.

Reality finally hit me. Driving on this road was a terrible idea. I could feel Jake's bewilderment switching to anger.

I hopped out of the car to try and move snow out of the way of the tires. Jake took the driver's seat and tried to maneuver the car while I shoveled and pushed. The more we tried, the deeper the car sank, and the more stuck we became. It was useless to struggle anymore—everything we tried made the situation worse. We were undeniably stuck. The car was sitting at a diagonal with the left wheels buried halfway into the snow. We had to give up. I let go of all my plans, and we called for help.

Jake's dad came to the rescue with a truck and his reliable good spirit. He almost got his own vehicle stuck, but his positive energy seemed to help in more ways than one. He smiled and joked a bit, then pulled our car back to the main road.

We drove away from that perilous situation with our minds spinning. I was grateful and shaken all at once. The energy between us was thick and heavy, and it was a quiet drive to pick up the kids from the bus stop.

Of course, now the story is hilarious as we recall all the emotions and my stupidity. I was so absorbed by my plan to go for a hike that I couldn't see the truth of the current situation. It wasn't until we were sliding out of control that I started realizing what I was doing. Then, struggling to fix the situation by continuing to drive only made things worse. I had to wake up to reality, abandon my plans, and let go of trying to control a situation that was headed for disaster.

Down a Familiar Road

When we joined the family business thirteen years ago, we turned off the metaphorical highway and onto a snow-covered, windy road. We had no idea what we were getting ourselves into, but we had all the best intentions.

The red flags were everywhere.

I had uneasy feelings from the start. I voiced my concerns to Jake, but the plans were already in motion. So I sat in the passenger seat and allowed our lives to turn onto the hazardous road.

We were all in.

Midwestern family farms are very exclusive. Bloodline, hierarchy, age, gender, and relations are everything. We were excited to be initiated and prove our loyalty and worth, but we were completely unaware of the bigger picture. We signed documents that we didn't read through carefully and didn't understand until years later. We were so focused on our plans for the future that we took our lives on this questionable path anyway.

We accepted being at the bottom of the hierarchy. As a woman, a wife, and an in-law (not a direct bloodline of the family business), I was not trusted with business decisions or ownership. I was "Mrs. Jacob Rieke." If something ever happened to Jake, no matter how many years of my life I gave to the farm, I was expected to walk away from the business and my home like it meant nothing to me. The forward momentum of our lives slowed to a stop, and we tried to carefully reverse to where we thought the path should be.

Jake was expected to work seven days a week, as many hours as his body would allow—through meal times, overnight if necessary, and be on call twenty-four seven. He rarely took any days off for holidays, vacations, or sick time. I was supposed to be his unpaid "helper." We tried to hit the accelerator and focused all our attention on getting back to the right path . . ..

But it only made things worse.

The farm owned and provided a house for us to live in, a car to drive, health insurance, and car insurance. Since we did not have a mortgage or large bills to pay, this would keep our paychecks and taxes low. It made sense at first, but as time went on, we realized that our friends were building their equity and could sell their homes or trade their cars when they were ready to upgrade. We had no home or car to our name. Our lives slid into a very uneasy angle.

Jake felt compelled to uphold his family legacy. He was honored to be the fifth generation to run the farm, and we wanted it to thrive for generations to come. All the generations before us inherited the business when the previous generation passed away. We were the first to try to buy the business as our elders retired. But the elders never retired. They held on to the majority of the shares while the value increased. Jake questioned the plan for transitioning the business more and more, but it was met with explanations about paying less taxes and a nonchalant, "You'll figure it out when we're gone."

The harder we worked, the more the company profited, and the harder it was for us to buy the family business. As years turned into a decade, the value doubled, and the potential for us to buy the company slowly slipped away. The situation became impossible. We had to completely let go of our plans and the path.

Losing Our Way

Looking back, I can see how clearly my subconscious was yelling, "What are you doing?!" But I stuffed down the emotions and tried to fulfill my roles and duties. It was the same for Jake. We did everything possible to ignore the red flags, numb the pain, and avoid the sense of impending doom.

We used food to soothe our anxiety—the more sugar the better. We drank alcohol to ease the depression and catch a small glimpse of fun. We started filling up the giant farmhouse with stuff to distract us. We stayed up late watching screens to switch off our brains at night. Then we used caffeine and ibuprofen the next morning to combat the exhaustion and headaches.

Numbing the pain was one of the ways we tried to stay on the path. **We thought the coping mechanisms would help, but the momentary distractions only made the situation worse. Not only did it put our health at serious risk, but our brains were in a fog. We were too tired and dazed to think straight, let alone question our situation and find a way out.**

So we had kids.

Our two girls bring us more joy and love than we could have ever imagined. However, it did nothing to solve our problems. In fact, our mindset toward parenting made our situation worse and the problems compounded. We began living only for our kids, and we took ourselves completely out of the equation. We were told that "a farm is a great place to raise a family." So we had to stick this out for our kids. Our own future no longer mattered.

We were scared to lose our place on the farm because it provided us with a home, a vehicle, health insurance, car insurance, and a monthly wage. *How would we replace all those things quickly enough with two kids to support?*

The sunken cost kept growing. The more blood, sweat, and tears we poured into this life, the more invested we were in making it work. There was no way we could ever get out of here; we had already put too much of our lives into it. We had no choice but to continue. Someday we would reap what we were sowing.

What weighed most heavily on our shoulders was the family legacy. We were proud to be the fifth generation, and we were not going to let anyone down. No matter what. We filled the roles we had accepted and did not believe we could ever change our minds.

These were all the ways we were driving that metaphorical car back and forth in the snow, trying to keep going and make this life work.

We bought more things to keep us distracted, but it only weighed our house down. We ate more to keep us distracted, but it only weighed our bodies down. We drank more to keep us distracted, but it only weighed our minds down. We kept ourselves crazy busy with work so we didn't have to acknowledge the bigger picture and treacherous path.

When we accidentally had quiet moments—that is when the depression set in. Depression was harder than anything else. It felt isolating and overwhelming, and we quickly jumped to anything that would mask it again. The depression was dark and heavy, and we were too afraid to feel our unhappiness. Stay busy. Stay numb. Just keep moving, and everything will be fine. We kept running away instead of facing the darkness.

We were in a downward spiral.

In hindsight, it is easy to see that our depression and anxiety were a result of the bigger picture. We didn't have to be scared that there was something wrong with us. It was just the opposite. The depression was a healthy reaction. It was trying to tell us that we needed to change our lives. Our thoughts and emotions were doing exactly what they needed to do, we just had to listen to them.

It is so easy to be completely unaware of everything around you and ignore the signs. We can become so set on an idea inside our minds, all the while going down the wrong path with blinders on.

Everyone has blind spots. Everyone thinks what they are doing is rational. But many people rarely look truthfully at the present moment. It's hard to see past all the thoughts, limiting beliefs, judgments, and expectations swirling around in your head. Jake and I now constantly ask ourselves and each other, "What blind spots do we have?" But how do you find your blind spots when you are looking through your own lens *with those blind spots*?

One way is to acknowledge and accept the feeling of being stuck or depressed. Your emotions are trying to communicate with you. Don't mask them, and don't distract yourself from them. You don't have to feel embarrassed or ashamed if your mental health is signaling that you need to make a change. Accept your emotions and learn from them. Start searching for all the red flags and blind spots.

Unfortunately by the time you realize that you are stuck, there is going to be a lot to undo and even more to completely let go. And you did it all to yourself with the best of intentions. But it's going to be okay. It may be hard at first, but it will be worth it. You will come out on the other side as a stronger, better person. We want to help you through it.

How Are You Stuck?

The more we tell our story, the more people open up to us about their feelings of being stuck or depressed. There are so many reasons that people feel obligated to stay in their current situation, even if they realize they aren't happy. There is a tremendous amount of guilt and limiting beliefs that prevent people from taking the right path or from letting go of the wrong one. Here are a few of the reasons we have found, but I am sure there are many more.

Fulfilling an identity

As we get older, our world and its possibilities seem to shrink. The decisions we have made start to harden our lives into a narrow corridor. We can't see the options and choices we have for learning, growing, and changing. We think being an adult means staying the same for the rest of our lives, so we lean into the singular identity of a career or a relationship and allow the stereotypes to lead us.

When Jake and I chose to join his family's business, we accepted the roles of Farmer and Farmer's Wife. I thought this meant I had to be an agreeable wife, a loyal farmhand, a dedicated homemaker, and a busy mom. We let the responsibilities and stereotypes consume us, while everything else faded into the background. We did that for so long that we completely forgot who we were. When we finally let go and moved away from the farm, we started remembering so many things about ourselves that we had repressed for thirteen years. Jake's love of motorcycles is just one of the many examples. He let his motorcycle sit in a forgotten shed for so long that it was totaled. When we moved away from the farm and his farmer identity, his joy of motorcycles was rekindled and he bought a new one.

Peer pressure

Expectations and judgment from our family, friends, neighbors, and communities have a big impact on us. We want to fit in. We want to prove ourselves. We want to succeed. We want to be liked. We want to please everyone. So we change ourselves to be the person we think they want us to be. We let it control how we act, how we live, and even how we think. It holds us back from doing unique things that bring us joy, thinking for ourselves, and becoming the people we were meant to be. When we allow peer pressure to change who we are, it can lead to resentment or depression.

When we first moved to the farm, I wanted to paint a black accent wall in our farmhouse dining room. The handful of people that I dared to mention this to convinced me it was not acceptable. So I tried painting it a few different colors that were deemed normal, but

I disliked them all. Luckily my mom was always cheering on my bold choices. With her encouragement, I finally let go of what everyone else thought and just painted it black. And we loved it.

Generational gaps

As beautiful as it is to learn from the generations that come before us, it must be balanced with growth. Learning and evolving is a natural rhythm. We cannot restrict our lives to doing things the way they have always been done. This is especially difficult with families, when there are generations who are locked into their ways and resent anything that challenges them.

Even after a decade of proving ourselves and managing the family farm successfully, we were never allowed to make any big changes or transfer ownership completely. Jake had ideas like strip-till farming, cover crops, increasing crop variety, transitioning land into a solar farm, building greenhouses, and so many more. Since Jake was never trusted to fully take over the family business, it eventually broke him down. Since the conventional farming methods we were expected to follow did not align with my core values, it eventually broke me down.

Security

We feel dependent on steady jobs, money, insurance, and relationships—they rule our choices and our world. These security blankets prevent us from taking risks and making changes to our lives. In the moment, the risk seems much scarier than continuing on as always. But if safety results in depression, then it is the other way around. Continuing with normal becomes a bigger risk.

Jake and I were scared. The farm provided all these things for us, and it could also take them away. Since we did not want to seem greedy, we didn't question Jake's low salary or lack of a retirement account. The farm would provide, and we should be grateful. We did not live intentionally toward independence, so it made letting go that much harder.

Sunk cost

When you put time, effort, finances, and resources into your current situation, it can be very difficult to give up your investment. But the longer you continue, the more sunken cost there will be. If something is not serving you, then you must let it go, no matter how much you have put into it. The longer you resist, the more toxic it will become.

We devoted over a decade of our lives to the family farm, thinking that it would eventually be ours. Letting go felt like all that time, energy, blood, sweat, and tears were stolen from us. But now we know that the journey was our reward, not the material possession of it. The experience transformed us, and there was no sunken cost that could be taken away. Personal growth was the most important investment we ever made and we wouldn't trade it for anything.

Children

Parents are wonderful at putting their kids' happiness before themselves. But maybe what kids need the most is for their parents to pursue what's meaningful to them. Then they show up in the best way possible.

We have two amazing daughters. We were doing all the right things to raise them for success, but there was no joy in our household. When we finally realized that if we focused on our own health and purpose, then it had a natural ripple effect on our kids. Yes, changing school systems or moving to a new community might be a challenge for them to face. But imagine how much easier that change was than trying to live with upset or depressed parents for their entire lives.

Limiting beliefs

Limiting beliefs are the most challenging way to be stuck. They are our minds playing tricks on reality and the world of possibility. They are so ingrained into our lives that uncovering them is a never-ending task. They are so ingrained into our culture that questioning them can be scary.

Jake and I have found so many limiting beliefs hiding in our lives and our minds. We lived according to them for many years, and we are slowly peeling away the layers. One of the biggest limiting beliefs that we had to overcome, and continue to fight against, is that we aren't good enough.

Coping mechanisms

Unhealthy coping mechanisms can turn into daily habits or addictions. They take a toll on your body and mind and make it even harder for you to free yourself. You deplete the energy and clarity needed to get yourself out of a toxic situation and into the life you deserve.

The more Jake and I relied on unhealthy habits, the more our tolerance grew, and the more we had to use them. They made it impossible to see the truth, believe in ourselves, and make changes. We were exhausted physically, mentally, and emotionally.

Learned helplessness

All the ways that we become stuck lead to learned helplessness. We believe that we are victims of our own lives. We can't imagine a way out. We give up on ourselves and our ability to take action toward a better life. This is the mindset that we must change.

This is the mindset that we were finally able to break free from. This is why we feel compelled to write this book. We want you to take back your power. You are not a victim.

Finding Ourselves

With so many excellent ways to be stuck, how do you wake up and become aware that your current path is treacherous? How do you see the truth that you aren't going anywhere, just metaphorically sinking down further into the snow?

The wake-up call is different for everyone. People have different experiences and levels of intuition. Watch for all the signs pointing you in the right direction, as well as all the red flags trying to warn you against the wrong direction. Many of us endure the stress of the wrong path for way too long. It took Jake and me a decade to slowly wake up. But we are grateful that we didn't spend another ten years—or the rest of our lives.

Since then, it has been a constant cycle of acknowledging the red flags and signs, eliminating blind spots and limiting beliefs, and pivoting our lives. Everything we have learned and all the ways we were able to change are included in the chapters to come.

The typical American lifestyle keeps us so busy that we can't hear ourselves over the noise. There is always something to do, something to consume, something to watch. We are in a hectic daze that gets us nowhere. And we eagerly jump to easy ways to mask the painful emotions. We rarely stop to clear our head and truly listen to ourselves.

We want you to slow down and pay attention to the quiet moments, not the busy ones. Allow the signs and red flags to guide you. Use the feeling of being stuck to become aware of your situation and how you got yourself into it. You can learn, grow and become a new person.

Use The Brilliant Life Journey action steps in this book to find and trust yourself again. You are not stuck. You can let go and change your path at any moment.

CHAPTER 3

From Crisis to Catalyst

Our downward spiral finally reached a breaking point. The stress, the responsibilities, the expectations, and the mistreatment had built up so high that we were pushed to our edge.

It was time for a midlife crisis—Jake's was first.

After working for more than a decade as a laborer for his family farm and feeling stuck in every way possible, Jake finally found the courage to stand up for himself. He called his family member and told them we could not continue with business as usual. We had to figure out the transition plan for the family farm, or it was time for us to start a new career.

It's somehow shocking, yet not surprising, when people's reactions reveal their true feelings. You realize you have always felt the undertones lurking. The shallow shell of "Minnesota Nice" had cracked open, and there was no going back.

So Jake called mediators, financial advisors, tax advisors, farm transition experts, and eventually legal counsel. For a year and a half, the consultants came up with multiple ways to compromise and keep the farm legacy going. The company's value kept climbing and had now more than doubled since we began working for the business. We felt powerless and trapped in an impossible situation. We compromised to the point of cringing and offered up deal after deal. Each one was rejected.

It felt like the world turned against us, and we were blamed for everything. There were rumors and lies flying around the small community, hate mail coming directly to our mailbox and email, social media posts meant to harm our reputations, and business meetings where we endured the wrath and false accusations made right to our faces. We tried to stay calm and not fight back, which seemed to enrage them even more.

Thankfully, we had Jake's parents supporting our efforts. They witnessed the absurd backlash and absorbed the attack alongside us. Between the four of us, we owned the majority of the farm business. Legally we could have taken the company in any direction we wanted. But our conscience wouldn't allow it.

Why were we trying so hard to make this work? Because it was all we knew.

Cue *my* midlife crisis, which I proudly renamed my "midlife awakening."

Watching Jake go through his midlife crisis was empowering, and I was ready. I booked a week-long yoga retreat in Costa Rica and braced myself. It did not disappoint.

I found distance, clarity, a warm community of open-minded women, healthy practices for my body, mind, and spirit, a breakdown, and a breakthrough. I finally realized the farm was toxic to my soul. The identity of "Farmer's Wife" was toxic to my soul. The escalating situation with our extended family and the business transition was toxic to my soul. We had to put an end to it all.

I called Jake from Costa Rica. He answered, and a lump formed in my throat. I couldn't speak.

But he somehow knew everything.

From the silence, Jake said, "I know."

Without any explanation and from thousands of miles away, he could sense my monumental shift. We were united.

We were ready to let go of everything and jump into the unknown. We were ready to let go of the difficult path that we were trying so hard to figure out. We were ready to let go of the future we thought was so fixed. We were ready to let go of the farm, our identities, our home, our careers, our community, and especially the people who were trying to keep us there. We were in our early forties and ready to start our lives over again. It was frightening. It was thrilling. It was liberating.

One Choice, Infinite Impact

In the movie *The Matrix*, Neo reaches his edge. He questions the reality that is no longer serving him. He starts to follow his curiosity and trust his intuition. Then he is faced with a choice: **a blue pill to send him back to the life that was dragging him down, or a red pill to jump into the unknown in search of truth and purpose.**

The blue pill means a return to the American trance. It means numbing your feelings and increasing your threshold for stress. It means forgetting who you really are deep down.

The red pill is terrifying. It is stepping away from everything you know. You don't know the ending. You don't know who you will be.

You must follow your own intuition, your own passion, and your own unique calling.

Jake and I took the red pill, and there was no going back.

When I returned from Costa Rica, people asked, "How was it?"

And I responded, "Life-changing."

Everything was exactly the same, yet somehow completely different. We saw the world from a new perspective. Our situation had not changed, but our minds had opened to the possibilities. We no longer felt stuck. Taking the red pill was not just scary, it was exhilarating and full of hope.

We slowly started breaking the news that we were going to resign from our positions in the family business and move off the farm site. It was met with a lot of resistance and hostility, but it no longer controlled us.

The farmland would be divided and auctioned off to pay the owners. The houses, hog barns, machinery, vehicles, and everything the business owned would go up for auction. We started packing our personal possessions and throwing away all the junk that we had accumulated over the years.

The hateful comments, rumors, and lies continued coming at us. We did our best to dodge the bullets, just like Neo. But there were still battles we had to endure. It was as if the Universe was solidifying our decision to leave a toxic situation.

As the auction date was closing in, we had to open our house and farm site for potential buyers to walk through. The auction company planned it for a day when we happened to be out of town. In fact, we were on a trip with our kids to a personal development conference in Columbus, Ohio.

But while we were gone listening to motivational speakers, Jake's extended family took advantage of the situation back home and swooped in. The auction company called and told us everything they witnessed in our business office and in our house. It would have been impossible to believe them, except the security camera footage confirmed it all. We felt violated and bewildered, and to be completely honest, we were terrified. People who we loved and trusted were no longer recognizable. But the most unnerving part was when the security camera was intentionally covered for ten minutes.

The stories from that day, the camera footage, the missing camera footage, the threatening behavior, and hateful messages turned our lives upside down. If our own family could cross the line of what we thought was possible, then *where was the line?!*

We no longer felt safe sleeping in our own house, we no longer felt safe going for a jog in our neighborhood, we no longer felt safe walking down our own driveway, we no longer felt safe stepping a few feet away from our children or each other.

When our trip to Columbus ended, we had no choice but to return to the Matrix and retrieve our cat, finish packing our personal possessions, and help coordinate the auction sale. We called everyone we could to help us pack and escape as quickly as possible. We booked a temporary place to stay while we finalized the purchase of a new home.

It was the most surreal experience of our lives. We could not believe that it was once the reality in which we had been a willing participant. We were now witnessing the Matrix from the outside.

Sparks of Freedom

We moved to a nearby town about twenty miles away. It was close enough to the farm where we could complete the auction and legal work from a safe distance. Thankfully, this was the town where our kids had transferred for school, so they wouldn't have to overhaul their lives in the midst of trauma. Their friends, teachers, and school days could provide a stable foundation for them. In fact, they were excited that they didn't have a long bus ride to school anymore.

This was also the town where my mom and sister lived. This was where we went for music lessons, fitness classes, doctor appointments, and grocery shopping. Why didn't we see this incredible opportunity before? The veil of our Matrix reality had blinded us so much that even obvious options had been hiding.

We found a duplex for sale in a beautiful neighborhood near the school, clinic, and library, and within biking distance of everything else. We rented the other half of our duplex to help pay the mortgage. It was a house hack to ease the burden of starting on our own. Everything seemed so clear now that we had taken the red pill.

The leap into the unknown was the scariest, most challenging thing we ever did. It took some serious suffering, and then courage, for us to finally close our eyes and let go of our current life and the future we had all planned out. But once we did, it was the most freeing feeling we had ever experienced. The weight of our lives lifted.

We realized that we were not meant to be the fifth generation of a family farm. We were meant to be the next Generation Zero. We are following in the footsteps of the previous Generation Zero who immigrated to America.

We are continuing the family legacy, not of a farm business, but in search of a better life. In search of adventure, purpose, and meaning. We visited the cemetery and thanked our ancestors who had the courage to let go of their lives and search for a new one. We know they are proud of us.

We are starting a completely new life in a new reality.

Our "midlife crisis" was so much better than the dark depression that preceded it. In fact, I don't believe it was a crisis at all, but an end to the crisis we were feeling inside. The "crisis" is a label that other people use when they are surprised, confused, or even jealous of spontaneity and confidence. I believe it should be called a "midlife awakening" when you emerge from the dark despair of a meaningless life and rebel against the norm.

Change Agents

Moving from our depressed, stuck selves into a bright, limitless future required three events to unfold. We had reached the **edge** of what we were willing to put up with, declared an **ultimatum** for change, and found the courage to **let go** of everything and jump into the unknown.

How much will you endure before reaching your **edge**?

Are you ready to stand up for yourself and declare an **ultimatum**?

Do you have the courage to **let go**?

No one can make these decisions for you. No one can force you to be ready. But when you decide to take the red pill and leave the Matrix, a beautiful world will be waiting for you.

All the Universe's secrets have been spelled out in black and white, in thousands of ways, in thousands of voices, and for thousands of years. Every spiritual text and every personal development book tries to point us to the same answers. Everyone is trying to help us see through the illusion that our egos have us ensnared in.

But no number of stories, books, or authors can make you understand the sensation that the words are pointing to. **You are the one who must open your mind enough to free yourself.**

Find Your Edge

Everyone has a unique threshold of what they put up with. People have remarkable levels of patience, tolerance, and a willingness to suffer. We get caught in repeating patterns that slowly wear us down, and it is difficult to see the way out.

Jake and I found ourselves relearning lessons that we had learned decades earlier, and it felt like déjà vu:

* When I was young, I hated living outside of town, isolated from my friends. But as an adult, I had accepted living on a farm, separated from others. I had to relearn the lesson of needing community.

* When I was in high school, I was constantly longing for a larger school system with more opportunities for art and music. As an adult, I started sending my own kids to the exact same school system with the same problems which had been amplified over time. I had to relearn the lesson of choosing opportunities over limits.

* When I was in college, I wanted to broaden my perspective and see the world. As an adult, I moved back to rural Minnesota and was planning to live in the same house for

the rest of my life. I had to relearn the lesson of seeking adventure.

I could go on and on. It was like I was living in a time warp. My life was stuck learning the same lessons I had learned long ago. I could hit rewind on my life and hardly see any difference, except this time I had children of my own.

But now, I was finally ready to be done with these lessons. I was ready to move on.

If you have found your edge, then you are ready to disrupt the loops that you have been stuck in your entire life. Only you can decide when you have had enough and when you are ready to break free.

Declare an Ultimatum

Declaring an ultimatum is like rejecting the blue pill. When you decide that you can no longer return to the same existence day after day, you must make a stand. The ultimatum can be big or small. It can be a promise to yourself, like taking better care of your health. It can be finally pursuing a goal that has eluded you. It can be related to your career, your family, your habits, or whatever area of your life isn't serving you. Or it could be absolutely everything—like us.

When Jake made that phone call to his family, he was finally standing up for himself and rejecting the blue pill. It was our *ultimate* ultimatum. Enough. No more of this. We did not see the other options yet; we just knew that things could not continue as they were.

Uncover the Courage to Let Go

It took two years from the moment that Jake declared his ultimatum to the moment we could finally let go. It took that amount of time to finally see the red pill and find the courage to choose it. Those two years were a frenzy of soul-searching, personal development, and self-investment. But that was when the magic happened. That was when we learned the steps to our Brilliant Life Journey. While negative energy was building up around us, we were building up positive energy within us.

All that positive energy created a rapid cascade of change. It swirled around us and impacted everything within our vicinity. Our reality, which had become so stale and meaningless, lit up like fireworks. It changed our perspective, our attitude, and our understanding of the circumstances. We started coming up with creative solutions for our future and seeing opportunities everywhere. We let go of all the ridiculous rules and limits we placed on ourselves.

The courage to let go does not mean that you should immediately quit your job, move to a new place, or disown your family and friends. We spent several years building our independence by saving money, investing in real estate, investing in our future goals with classes and experiences, networking with people who could help us, and experimenting with new ideas. We got laser-focused and intentional about where we were spending our time, money, and energy and what we were putting into our bodies and minds.

Those two years were a process of building confidence and independence, unlocking the mental chains that were keeping us stuck, and preparing ourselves to let go and finally take the red pill. And it was only the beginning of our Brilliant Life Journey.

Leaving the Past Behind

The veil of the Matrix is not limited to family businesses or Midwestern farms. That was just the situation we happened to be trapped in. And after stepping out of our Matrix, we could look at our previous reality with a new lens. The rules we used to take so seriously now seemed ridiculous. Here are just a few examples of what we accepted:

* Saving money on the most trivial expenses mattered more than anything else. It could come at the cost of time, safety, sleep, health, or lifespan.
* Running a farm meant doing everything yourself. Hiring contractors or employees meant you were lazy.
* Manual labor was honorable. The dirtier you got, the more you proved yourself.
* Exercising and prioritizing your health were guilty pleasures. That time and energy should go toward work.
* The generations before us know everything, and we know nothing.
* The family legacy was the farmland and the job, not the people.

Now we shake our heads in disbelief. There is no one to blame but ourselves. We allowed all these things to happen and the mindsets to take hold. We chose to put ourselves into that situation, and we chose to let it consume us. We chose to accept the identities of the dutiful fifth-generation farmer and wife. It was easier than thinking for ourselves and taking responsibility for our circumstances. We needed the pain to grow and finally take ownership of our lives. We are truly grateful for the suffering because it pushed us to our edge and finally freed us.

The entire experience has generated new levels of understanding and empathy within us. The Matrix we had been living in was created over many years and many generations. At one point in time, the original values, beliefs, social rules, and technologies may have served the people incredibly well. They were probably born out of necessity, but over time have become illogical. The family farm and the generation before us were caught in that reality too. By learning from our own introspection, we've discovered compassion for their life situations and their actions toward us. It was not their choice or their fault for treating us the way they did.

But even though we feel free from the situation that we struggled with for thirteen years, we are far from finished with our journey. We continue to uncover more levels on our Brilliant Life Journey every day. We sometimes find ourselves reverting to old tendencies and old mindsets. We find new layers of trauma to work through and new levels of joy to express. Writing this book and explaining the steps of our Brilliant Life Journey is helping us stay connected to the growth we are searching for. It reminds us of all the empowering ways to take back control of our minds and our lives.

The most exciting part is that there is always another layer of the Matrix to discover.

Get ready to change your life. Phase 1 starts now.

PHASE 1

Contemplate

CHAPTER 4

Contemplate

L ike many adults our age, Jake and I used to drink a lot of alcohol. It was our go-to for every occasion, big or small, happy or sad. We loved hosting themed parties with special cocktails, going camping with a fridge full of beer and seltzer, and visiting wineries and breweries. We'd crack open a bottle at the first sign of sunshine or mix a drink for an impending snowstorm. We had an impressive liquor cabinet and an ever-growing collection of excuses to indulge.

Jake, with his eclectic taste in music, was usually designated as the DJ. We would turn up the music and allow the songs to melt away our inhibitions. One of my favorite songs was called "Jordan B Peterson's Drinking Song" by Akira the Don. I couldn't help myself but dance and sing along every time. It had a catchy beat and lyrics that were fun to belt out when you had a drink in your hand.

[Chorus]
Alcohol
It's an interesting drug

Alcohol
It's a hell of a drug
Alcohol
It's a great drug
But the problem is
It's a great drug[1]

Until one fateful day, when I listened to the song sober. The lyrics, once a source of amusement, now felt unsettling. I shook the feelings away. *No need to overanalyze.*

So why stop?
Well, you do stupid things when you're drunk
You hurt yourself
you compromise your health
it's really hard on the people around you
You tend to turn into a liar and it screws up your life[2]

Over time, the lyrics slowly started to seep into my awareness and haunt me. I listened to the entire album sober, each song with its own intriguing message. The album became my go-to playlist for jogging.

The real surprise came when Jake told me that Jordan B Peterson is a psychologist. *What??* Akira the Don had woven his recorded lectures into music. By listening to that song over and over, I had accidentally brainwashed myself. But in reality, I guess it was the opposite of what we consider brainwashing because it released my mind from alcohol's control.

That song played a pivotal role in my journey to sobriety. For my part, it took curiosity, an open mind to question my current lifestyle, and clarity. Once I did, there was no turning back. Clear and honest contemplation was the key that unlocked everything.

Time and Space for Self-Awareness

Jake and I had to dig deep during our Contemplation phase to gain an accurate picture of ourselves. It took a lot to dismantle the walls we had built around ourselves. I could see Jake's suffering clearly, but it took longer to acknowledge my own. I remember asking him throughout the most difficult years, "Are you sure this is how you want to spend your life?" And he would struggle to answer, "Yes . . .." with different amounts of reservation and doubt. But I did not even consider asking myself the same question. I thought I was fine.

Denial was a tough shell to crack.

Our Contemplation process will guide you through everything we did to gain that honest awareness. We experimented with a wide variety of ideas and practices, many of which we still incorporate today. We hope you will try the ones that resonate with you. Then try some more. Or if you are like Jake and me, never stop trying and see what sticks around the longest.

Our Contemplation phase can be divided into five areas:

1. Quiet the outside world
2. Slow down your life
3. Understand yourself
4. Assess your current situation
5. Widen your perspective

These five areas were all very important to get our lives turned in a better direction, and they are still important for us today. Writing this book is helping us remember some of the things we did and what we need to bring back into our lives again. It's also a great reminder that there is no finish line. The goal is to simply be on the journey.

1. Quiet the Outside World

Tuning out the busy world was a natural first step for us because it was the lowest-hanging fruit. Living out in the countryside made some of these changes pretty natural, and others were just a happy coincidence. But then we started feeling the results, and it gave us momentum. By quieting the unnecessary external commotion, Jake and I started creating space for our inner voices to finally emerge.

Tune Out the News Frenzy

This was one of the first things we did, although initially it was by accident. Jake and I used to be news junkies, and we thrived on being informed, up-to-date, and very opinionated. We listened to the news all day long: at home, at work, in the car, anywhere. But divisive politics, fear-mongering, and incessant news organizations left us exhausted. Out of necessity, we reduced our news consumption and gradually cut out our daily exposure completely. The relief was enormous! We gained so much more brain space, and the negative spins no longer brought us down. Now, when someone in our life gets worked up about a particular story or political view, it is liberating not to feel trapped in the fervor. Staying informed about what is happening in the world is still important to us, but we don't allow the fear and tension to affect our daily stress levels. Word-of-mouth is now our preferred method of receiving news, and it's all we need.

I realize this may be difficult, but please just try it. Stop watching, listening, and reading the news, and delete the notifications from your devices. If the idea of giving up the news seems crazy or irresponsible, just try it for a few weeks and see if you notice a difference in how you feel.

Limit Social Media

Social media can be even more invasive than the news, and is exponentially more addicting. Jake is particularly susceptible to watching videos on YouTube. It always begins innocently enough, and he is usually trying to learn something. But one video leads to the next, and all of a sudden it's an hour later. Then the kids and I are knocking on the bathroom door wondering when it's our turn. He recently deleted the social media apps from his phone and we are appreciating the shorter bathroom line.

Delete your social media apps if they are unnecessary, make you feel bad about yourself, or create addictive behaviors. If you can't give them up completely, set time limits for the individual apps or restrict yourself from using them on certain devices like your phone.

Set Screen Time Boundaries

When Jake and I jump into work emails or computer tasks when we first wake up, it can affect our mood for the entire day. The same goes for sleeping. If I watch a movie right before bed, my mind gets riled up. By limiting screens during these critical times, we now control the trajectory of our day and the quality of our sleep.

Eliminate screens for the first and last hour of each day.

Implement a Digital Detox

Our kids love playing video games on their tablets. No surprise there! However, we have noticed that the longer they play, the worse their mood is when we make them stop. It's almost like the negative energy starts to build up inside of them but doesn't show its ugly face until the trance of the screen is cut from their view. The solution we found is to allow small increments of time (usually 15–30 minutes). And if they do get the rare opportunity to play longer, then we usually make them go outside or do something active afterward. Seeing this phenomenon in our kids has made us realize that we are exactly the same way. Jake and I need frequent breaks from our computers just as much as they do. Our headaches, body aches, and fatigue vanish and our mental focus and moods drastically improve.

Take regular breaks from your screens and get some fresh air, stretch your body, read a book, etc. If you are really brave, try a three-day, tech-free vacation to clear your mind. It can be easier if you go somewhere without all the temptations. Camping is a great choice!

Enjoy the Silence of Nature

Seasonal depression is real, and it hits Minnesota hard. During the cold, dark days of winter, we rarely get outside. When we compare how lethargic we feel in the wintertime to how energized we feel in the summertime, it is shocking. We have finally accepted that moving to a warmer climate is now priority number one. Getting out into nature is one of the most therapeutic things we can do. We like going outside for almost any reason, but canoeing is one of our favorite activities. We prefer the smaller rivers and lakes, and I love the way the canoe glides silently over the water.

Get outside as much as you can. Whether it's hiking through a park, sitting in the grass, or watching the sunrise, reconnect with the natural world to find silence and stillness.

Find a Quiet Community Space

When we lived on a farm with a big house, quiet spaces were easy to find—but it was so isolated that our loneliness closed in. Now we live in a tiny two-bedroom apartment in town and we have the opposite problem. In both scenarios, our solution was the library. It was the perfect balance between finding community and a peaceful atmosphere. It could comfort us when we were lonely, or provide space for us when we needed some quiet time alone. We go there to read, work, play, craft, or join classes and groups. The library is our go-to in almost every situation.

Find a pleasant community space that gets you out of your home, offers a peaceful environment, and connects you with others. Besides a library, other options could be a church, community center, community garden, local park, coffee shop, book store, or restaurant. Find a place that brings you peace, joy, and connection.

2. Slow Down Your Life

In 2020, our lives went from 100 miles per hour to about 5 miles per hour. The COVID pandemic cleared our calendar overnight. The kids stayed home, and I quit my part-time job off the farm. All the lessons, classes, meetings, events, gatherings, and activities were canceled. It was a strange feeling. It was very lonely and difficult, and yet . . . very freeing. We forgot what it was like to just be at home together without anything to do.

The government shutdown came at an interesting moment in our personal development journey. This rare opportunity to slow down our lifestyle unintentionally slowed down our busy minds too. We discovered so many benefits to a more reasonable pace. We were better focused, more relaxed, better listeners, and more present with our kids. It helped us see our crazy lives from a new perspective. The COVID pandemic was a very scary and difficult moment in history, but we are grateful for some of the insights it provided us.

Single-Task

My mom tells a story about my dad's method for doing laundry when they were first married. Apparently he was the ultimate single-task master. My dad would take all the dirty laundry down to the basement and just sit next to the machines while they were running. He would patiently wait for them to finish, so he could switch the loads and complete the job before coming back upstairs. He did not run around the house finding other ways to fill his time. He sat. He waited. For a long time this story was funny to me, and we all thought it was ridiculous that he would just sit and wait when there were so many other things he could have been doing at the same time. Now I look back and admire his singular focus and stillness. It is a very rare quality.

Apparently I did not inherit this mindset because this one is especially hard for me. I always feel the need to maximize my time and fit as much into my day as possible. When I find a fifteen-minute window of time, I try to add in an errand. Or two. But then I am late for my original appointment and feel stressed out! Or, while I am working on one project, my mind starts planning the next one, and I don't complete the first one. I even start washing dishes while I am still eating a meal! I have to constantly call back my attention and try to focus on a single task. I know that I take on too many things at once, and even my life coach has to continuously remind me to stay laser-focused, which applies to short-term tasks and long-term goals as well.

Focus on a single task or goal at a time. Write a daily to-do list in the order that you want to complete your tasks, and stick to it. It can help to rate their importance and prioritize the most important tasks first. Let all the little things wait until later.

Breathe

Our daughter, Avery, had always been terrified of getting immunization shots. She worked herself up into a frenzy—her body got tense and she could hardly breathe. Sometimes she even cried, screamed, and made a run for it. But that just made the experience worse for her. When Avery got a little older, she learned how to use some deep breathing techniques to relax before the pinch, and it was much less painful and traumatic for her. In fact, Avery requested getting her ears pierced for her twelfth birthday. I was surprised and impressed, considering her history with needles. During the appointment, she used some intentional deep breathing to relax and prepare for the piercing, and she handled it like a pro. It is amazing how much our breathing can regulate our stress levels and body tension.

These are some easy breathing techniques you can use at any point during your day to calm down or relax:

* **Box breathing:** Inhale through the nose for four counts, hold for four counts, exhale through the nose for four counts, and hold for four counts. Repeat as many times as you like.

* **Three-part Breathing:** Hold one hand on your stomach and one hand on your chest and breathe through your nose.

Inhale and focus on expanding your belly, then inhale again and focus on expanding your rib cage, inhale a third time and expand your upper chest. Exhale and release in reverse order. Repeat as many times as you like.

Be Mindful

After I was diagnosed with pre-diabetes, I looked at the sugar content of all my food and was appalled. I had been consuming ridiculous amounts of sugar all day long without realizing it. Then to top it off, I would sit on the couch at night and zone out to the TV with a big bag of chocolate on my lap. So just becoming aware of my habits and the ingredients of what I was eating changed my actions. I started checking food labels and consciously choosing what to put into my body. I tried to focus on my food when I was eating instead of zoning out. It was my first step toward mindful eating and mindful living. It made me realize how important it is to pay attention to everything you are doing and to choose how you live with intention.

Pay more attention to yourself: thoughts, actions, words, and habits. Set reminders on your phone to stop throughout the day and observe what you are doing. Try to live with as much intention and awareness as you can.

Meditate

Like many people, we were once scared off by the word meditation. But when Jake's depression got too much for him to handle, he tried the "10-Percent Happier" app. It introduced him to meditation as a tool for mental and emotional health. After realizing that meditation wasn't as scary as it sounds, we began using the guided meditations on Apple Fitness+ and the Waking Up app.

It was fun to choose the length and theme of each session, it could be just a five-minute session about kindness or a twenty-minute session focused on calm. Meditation was whatever we wanted or needed it to be. Since then we have experimented with a variety of apps and meditation styles, and we try to incorporate some version of meditation into our daily routines. After meditating, we feel relaxed, refreshed, and ready to take on the rest of our day.

Begin with an open mind and give it a try, there is no wrong way. Start with just a few minutes in any comfortable position that works well for you. Personally I love lying down, but there is a risk of falling asleep so many people prefer to sit. There are so many online resources and apps, find something that sounds easy and resonates with you. Guided meditations are a great way to start.

Practice Yoga

Jake and I began using yoga stretches after jogging to loosen up and recover. We slowly incorporated it into our lives more and more. Not only did it increase our physical mobility, but at the same time it relaxed our minds and utilized breathing techniques. The movement satisfied my need to feel productive and decreased my stress levels. It incorporated so many important elements into one practice. Now, it's one of the most common remedies we prescribe in our household if someone is feeling tense, sore, overwhelmed, or stressed out.

Try some online yoga videos at home, or join a class in a nearby studio. Don't judge it based on your first awkward attempt; give it at least a month.

Feel Better

I used to keep my massage appointments a secret because I was worried that people would judge me for it. That sort of pampering was considered expensive and a waste of time. In the Midwest, especially within the farming culture, we are taught to feel guilty or ashamed of taking time out to care for ourselves. We think it signifies weakness, selfishness, or laziness. But these are the limiting beliefs that are preventing us from living our best life. When we take time to reduce our physical, mental, and emotional stress, we show up better for others, and it generates a positive ripple effect in all our lives. **It is never selfish to build and sustain the best version of you.**

Do something that makes you feel good every day. Take a bath, take a nap, sit outside, call a friend, get a massage, or simply enjoy a warm cup of tea in the evenings.

Be **Instead of** *Do*

I used to think that being a good mom was cramming our schedules full and keeping everyone busy. We would race from one thing to the next. But my kids were exhausted and they felt neglected even though we were together. What my kids really needed from me was to just relax and be present with them. They love when I can let go of the schedule and to-do list and I just sit, listen, or play along.

The person I admire most with this quality is Jake's mom. No matter what she is doing or how busy her life is, Janet can stop and make time for anyone. When she is hosting a house full of people, she will stop and play a game with one of her grandchildren. When she is in the middle of a task, she will stop and fully listen to anyone who starts up a conversation with her. When someone makes a request, she will drop everything and help them with it. When there are family members or friends in her presence, she will sit and be completely present with them.

Shift your focus from constant doing to simply being. Designate fifteen minutes per day and be present with someone you love.

3. Understand Yourself

When we served in the United States Peace Corps, we were encouraged to integrate into our tiny village in El Salvador and live like locals before starting any projects. It was very important to become a part of the community and understand their perspective.

We gained a lot of trust and respect by doing our best to fit into their way of life and follow as many cultural norms as possible, right down to the small details: Jake wore a white cowboy hat, and I used a *cesta* (a brightly colored, woven plastic basket) to carry everything. For two years, we ate tortillas and beans for most of our meals. We wore pants in the sweltering heat, showered by dumping cold buckets of water on our heads, and witnessed critters slithering and scampering through our rafters. We pushed ourselves to the limits, and it generated massive personal growth. It was awesome.

When we returned to rural Minnesota, we brought this mindset with us. We wanted to fit in with the locals and live by the cultural norms before offering our opinions. We wanted to understand their perspective and gain their trust and respect. Unfortunately, this mindset, which had served us so well for a temporary service in El Salvador, now made us completely vulnerable in a permanent situation with a family business. **We assimilated so well that we completely lost who we were. Over time, we forgot everything about ourselves.**

The past few years have been a discovery back to those people who signed up for the Peace Corps. *Who were they?* And as we have been getting in touch with those people again, we feel the pull to move back to Central America—something we would have never dreamed of five years ago.

The following exercises and mindset shifts are some of the ways that we have been getting to know and understand ourselves better.

Take a Self Assessment

The *Wheel of Life* is a common tool for evaluating all the different areas of your life separately and then seeing it as a whole. Essentially, you rate each of the categories with a score from 1–10 based on how satisfied you feel, then fill the values into a pie shape.

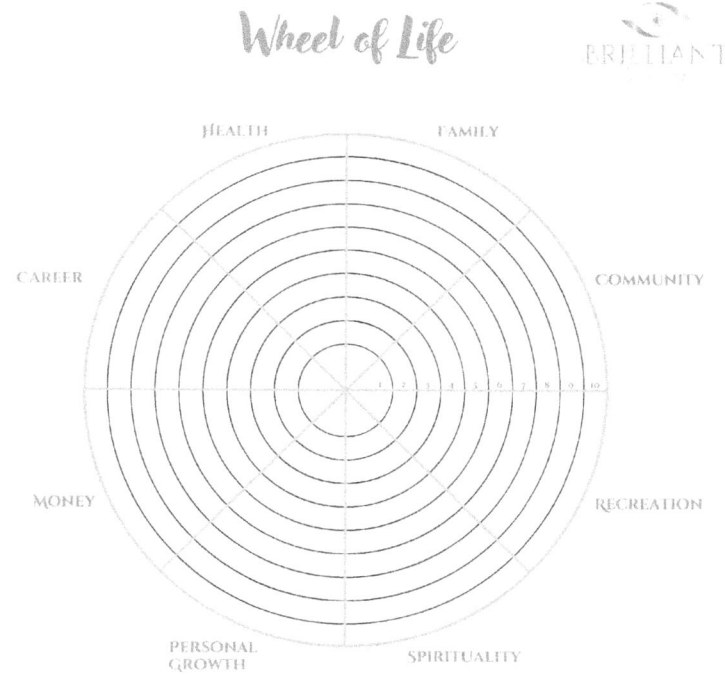

The goal is to have a balanced wheel that turns smoothly. The very low areas highlight where you may have deficits in your life and could benefit from extra attention. Some of the most common categories are health, relationships, career, spirituality, and personal development. For Jake and me, our most recent evaluations were very low in the areas of physical environment and family/friends, so we are focusing on increasing those values today.

Take a free online *Wheel of Life* assessment and evaluate which areas of your life to focus on. It may be tempting to prioritize them all since each category is important, but focus on just one or two at a time. You can find a free printable pdf at brilliantlifejourney.com/resources.

Understand Your Personality Type

The Enneagram is a tool that divides personality types into nine categories to understand desires, fears, motivations, and behaviors. There are many free online tests to guess which type is your most dominant, but the best way is to read a book or two about them and decide for yourself.

Knowing my most dominant personality type helps me understand what drives my actions and creates more self awareness. I appreciate the different personality types of my spouse and kids, and it has improved our relationships. I can better understand what motivates my family members, what frustrates them, and how to support them.

Read a book about the Enneagram to understand your dominant personality type and those of the people around you. I found a large selection of books on the subject at my local library, and one of the quick and easy reads that got me going was called *What's Your Enneatype?* by Liz Carver and Josh Green.

Evaluate your Values

Jake recently came across an exercise to help him structure his goals and life vision around his personal values. It was a set of Personal Values Cards—more than eighty different values, each printed on a small card. He sorted and narrowed them down into smaller and smaller piles to find his top five. We each took a turn, and it was very interesting to find our most essential values by matter of elimination. Many of the cards were important to us, but it was very insightful to find the final five that rose above the rest. Now we can make informed life decisions by prioritizing those values over everything else.

Try out a set of Values Cards and narrow them down to find your top five. If you prefer a physical set that you can sort by hand, there is a free, printable version online from the University of New Mexico. There is also a free app called *Personal Values Sort* that makes the process quick and easy. Whenever you are faced with a fork in the road, you can always return to this exercise and ask yourself which path is more in line with your most essential values. Make fulfilling those values your priority.

Learn the Language of Your Emotions

I was really excited to get my first tattoo, and I waited my whole life for something that seemed right. It finally came to me, and I scheduled a consultation with a local tattoo artist. After the appointment, I got in my car and had a strange sinking feeling. Something felt off.

I got home and was a little defensive about it when my family brought it up. Then, when Jake started looking at images to modify the design, I wouldn't even look at them. I went to bed that night feeling a little tense. Right before I fell asleep, I realized that all these sensations and emotions were telling me that the tattoo wasn't right.

I allowed myself to start researching and modifying the design again and found the perfect answer. My body relaxed and everything felt better again. My body had understood what was going on before my mind could explain it. I just had to listen.

Get curious about all the sensations that flow through your body. Notice when you have a gut feeling, a sinking feeling, a light-hearted feeling, goosebumps/chills, flushed/heat, stomach ache, headache, shallow or heavy breathing, the list goes on and on. Sometimes it helps to wait until you have a quiet, calm moment to reflect and evaluate their message to you.

Find Your Reflection in Others

When I tell my kids to clean up the house, I realize I need to clean up my own areas first. When I criticize my friends for not charging enough for their services, I realize it applies to my own career. When I get frustrated at other people for not focusing their time and energy well, it's because I am guilty of the exact same thing. When I give advice to my sister that she should never stop dreaming, I realize I need to give myself the same encouragement.

Stop and listen to yourself. If you are judging other people, make sure you are following the same advice that you are dishing out. View all of your critiques and suggestions as an opportunity for self-reflection. Anything that triggers you may be something you need to address in your own life.

Align with Authenticity

Sometimes I like to imagine that my life is being recorded for a reality tv show. Would my behavior change if I thought someone was watching? Would I eat differently? Dress differently? Look at myself in the mirror differently? Treat my family differently? Thinking about this scenario helps me to become more aware of my actions, words, facial expressions, and body language. I am more aware of how I am treating myself and if I am living in alignment with my values or compromising them. My goal is to live my most authentic life, whether I am alone, with others, or in front of a crowd.

Imagine your life as a reality tv show. Are you proud of the person who is captured on camera all day? Are you demonstrating what's truly important to you? Your unique authenticity is when your thoughts, feelings, words, and actions are aligned with your core values. Do whatever you can to find and live by that authenticity.

4. Assess Your Current Situation

When we moved off the farm and into town, we had no choice but to bring our cat named Partner. She had been an outdoor farm cat for eight years, and we weren't sure how she would handle living in a small space with the four of us. To our amazement, she adapted instantly, followed the new rules with dignity and precision, and enjoyed the extra attention. She quickly understood which yard was ours, stayed away from the busy road, and she sat politely at the door when she wanted to go in and out.

But the most surprising thing of all is that she became *playful*. Partner had never been playful on the farm. Now she was chasing after jingly balls, darting around corners, batting at toys, and even playing miniature pool with us. This was a side of Partner that we didn't know existed.

At the exact same time, we were experiencing the same phenomenon within ourselves. We were becoming playful, even Jake. Our kids started seeing a whole new side of us that they never knew existed. Now we laugh, joke, play, and have fun together. We don't take life so seriously, and the depth of our joy and love seems to be growing every day. The smaller living space did not confine us, instead it gave us more freedom to be ourselves and enjoy each other's company.

Our new living situation has opened up new levels to our personalities. And each level we find is more joyful and more intriguing than the last. Here are a few suggestions for evaluating where you are and planning for the future.

Determine Your Needs

Maslow's Hierarchy of Needs suggests that human needs can be categorized and shaped into a pyramid. You begin at the base and as you fulfill a need in your life, you rise up to the next category. Each level is important and builds a foundation for the levels above.

SELF-
ACTUALIZATION
Fulfill Potential
& Life Purpose

BRILLIANT

SELF-ESTEEM
Confidence, Respect,
Achievement

LOVE & BELONGING
Family, Friendship, Community, Connection

SAFETY NEEDS
Security, Health, Stability, Home, Money

PHYSIOLOGICAL NEEDS
Food, Water, Sleep, Shelter

Maslow's Hierarchy of Needs

When we were living on the farm, we were stuck at the level of safety and security. It had become so stressful that my hair started falling out and turning gray. After leaving the farm, Jake ended up seeking therapy to process all his deep emotional trauma. We could not worry about any of our other needs while this was dominating our lives.

But as soon as we moved away and started the healing process, we slowly began moving up the hierarchy to the level of Love & Belonging. We could see it in our cat, our kids, and ourselves.

Assess where you land in Maslow's Hierarchy of Needs and see if there is anything you can do to meet more of those needs and rise up to the next level. Be sure to address the foundational levels in the correct order before focusing upward. You can find a free printable pdf at brilliantlifejourney.com/resources

Ask Yourself: Am I Happy?

Jake was recently reorganizing all our digital photos. He was scrolling through all the years of our life and saw the evolution of our expressions and posture. During our years on the farm, we witnessed them falling into pure misery. It was shocking. Our eyes stared back at us with defeat and desperation. Why did it take ten years for us to see that within ourselves? Why is the suffering behind our eyes so clear to us in those old pictures, but was completely hidden from our awareness back then?

Look through photos of yourself throughout the years and find patterns of emotions and body language. Of course, most people take photos to show others how happy they are so the key is to look deep into your own eyes and find the true emotions. Or find photos of yourself where you are caught off-guard. What is your baseline expression and posture? Do you look happy?

Ask Yourself: Am I Living the Life that I Truly Want?

A few years ago, Jake bought me a book called *The Artist's Way* by Julia Cameron. As an artist searching to unlock creativity, I dove right in. The book was not at all what I expected and certainly not limited to artists, but it unlocked more than I could have ever imagined. One of the main elements is that you commit to writing "Morning Pages"— three pages of free writing every morning. I had not journaled much before that, and it made me uncomfortable to write all the thoughts that were going through my head. But afterward, I felt so much better. Sometimes it helped me let go, and sometimes it uncovered profound insights. I was acting as my own therapist. I started finding deeper answers for my life and my purpose. It helped me realize that I wasn't living the life I truly wanted and helped me discover what I needed to do and to change.

Free-write in a journal (start writing and let every thought come out on paper no matter how it sounds, it might start with, "I don't know what to write. I don't know what to write. I am just sitting here. This is silly and I feel uncomfortable. La, da, da…"). It works best to do this in the morning as soon as you can. If you want more, I highly recommend getting a copy of *The Artist's Way*.

Talk to Someone

One of my biggest resources and assets is Jake. We have deep, honest conversations almost daily. It helps us process all the situations and emotions that pass through our lives. The value those daily conversations bring to our lives is priceless. But we do need other people for their support too. When Jake's depression got too much for him, he spent quite a bit of time confiding in a close friend, his brother, and ultimately a therapist. I'm glad he found a support system because I would not have been able to help him through it all on my own.

Find someone you can talk to openly and honestly—a spouse, a friend, a family member, a life coach, a therapist, or all of the above. And if your depression or anxiety feels like too much to handle, please talk to a professional.

5. Widen Your Perspective

When Jake and I get stressed out, it's usually because our perspective has become too narrow. We get caught up in our own negative thoughts, our to-do list gets too long, our expectations of the day aren't met, or there is a single task that we resist. It's all the little things that bother us most. The stress that we allow it to create is not proportional to the importance that it has in our lives.

When we pause and look at the bigger picture, our priorities change. It can be really hard to do when you are caught up in the moment. Here are a few ways that Jake and I tap into this clarity.

Remember the Scare

We have had a few health scares over the years. Our first daughter, Avery, was born prematurely at thirty-one weeks in an emergency room. She was immediately airlifted to the nearest Children's Hospital, and I spent the next six weeks living on a futon in her hospital room. Nothing else mattered. All the things that stressed me out just hours before her birth (painting the nursery, finishing my to-do lists, drama with a coworker, my complexion, my hair, my maternity clothes) faded away into nothing.

There are certain situations that can realign our priorities in an instant. We become flooded with clarity when there is a health scare, an accident, a crisis, or the loss of a loved one. All of a sudden, our lives are shaken up and the little things no longer matter. These moments can come quickly, but can also be forgotten quickly. This is the clarity we want to tap into. This is what's really important.

Recall a time in your life when a situation scared your priorities straight. Remember what mattered and what didn't, and try to live your life in line with them.

Interview Your 100-Year-Old Self

The podcast host Lewis Howes gave this advice during one of his motivational talks. I think he referred to age 85, but I prefer to imagine age 100 instead. So, if you could talk to your 100-year-old self, what would they say? What guidance would they have? I use this imaginary scenario all the time when I have a difficult decision to make about my future. *What should I do? Is this worth the risk? What will I regret? What will I be proud of? What is important?*

I also like to think about it for everyday tasks as well. *Does this matter? What do I need to let go of? Is this a big deal or a small deal?* I try to imagine how my 100-year-old self would answer these questions and advise me. It helps widen my lens, shift my priorities, and live without any regrets.

Pretend you're having a conversation with your future self. Ask them anything. What advice would your 100-year-old self give you? Are you living your best life according to them? This could also be very insightful as a journaling prompt.

Write Your Own Eulogy

We have heard this advice from many sources, and it seems like the perfect way to end this chapter of Contemplation. If you were to sit down and write out your own eulogy, what would you want it to say? How would you want people to remember you? Are there non-negotiables that you want to accomplish before you are gone? Are there specific qualities that you want to shine above the rest?

Write your own eulogy, including all the ways you want people to remember you. Use the past tense as though all your dreams and goals have been achieved, and how you showed up as the person you wanted to be. Write the story of your life with no regrets.

You Need an Adventure

Jake and I used all the methods in our Contemplation phase over the course of many years so we could start thinking clearly. So we could wake up from our sad existence. So we could wake up to the reality surrounding us.

Eventually, we tuned out the noise, slowed down, started getting to know ourselves, evaluated the situation, and widened our perspective. We went from depressed zombies to hopeful, mindful human beings.

When our thoughts and perspectives changed, the drinking song was no longer haunting—it was inspiring. We noticed other lyrics in the song that encourage positive behavior. Besides the list of negative effects of alcohol, the song also gives a solution. And when you are in a clear and open state of mind, you can actually hear it.

No, you need an adventure, man
You need to get out there and have something to do
Something worth waking up for
That's the substitute for the addiction[3]

Once we had a strong conscious foundation built with our Contemplation phase, that's when our world started opening up.

We were awake.

We were ready for an adventure.

We were ready to find something that made life worth living sober.

That's when our Investigation phase was ready to begin.

That's when the fun began.

Knock, knock, Neo.

PHASE 2

Investigate

CHAPTER 5

Investigate

As the sun rose on a remote Greek island, Jake and I were out for an early morning jog. While absorbing the magic of the beautiful hills and the clear blue sea, a man walking on a nearby dirt path came into view. He was older but looked very healthy for his age with sun-tanned skin and comfortable, worn-out clothing.

He called out in a language we didn't understand, and Jake answered, "Sorry, I don't speak Greek."

The man answered in perfect English, "Then why don't you *learn* Greek?"

His authenticity caught us off guard, and his beaming energy drew us in. We felt a deep connection with this being who should have been a complete stranger. Time flew by as we spent the next hour and a half in deep conversation. We were so at ease in his presence that all of our inner struggles and truths came tumbling out.

We talked about spirituality, purpose, family, transitions, and finding our place in this world. We told him that we were searching for a new home. He gave us the most profound criteria of the three things we should consider:

* Do you like to breathe the air?
* Do you like the climate?
* Is there clean water?

It sounded so simple, so obvious, and yet . . . have we ever truly lived by them? For the past thirteen years, we would have said no to all three. Now that we are intentionally choosing a new place to live, they seem like the three most important elements to get right.

Spending the morning in deep conversation with that intriguing being made us feel like Alice in Wonderland. We were drawn in by an interesting character and began an unusual philosophical discussion. We allowed ourselves to be guided by child-like curiosity and forgot about our grown-up rules and schedule. We ended up missing our morning classes as our obligations seemed to fade into the background. And we were rewarded.

We later found out that this enlightened man was a true shaman. We had the good fortune of spending the morning with him, absorbing his wisdom. We knew we could use the shaman's advice to follow our most elusive white rabbit: relocating our family and finding our true purpose.

We would have never stopped to talk with this man a few years earlier. We would have never been out on a jog a few years earlier. And we would have never traveled to Greece a few years earlier. The white rabbit of curiosity, joy, and intuition took us to this time and place in our lives. Tapping into these skills over time seemed to be strengthening them.

Investigating and following our white rabbit started simply. Just like our Contemplation phase, it started with small steps that were neither intimidating nor difficult. Then we slowly built the muscles to look in new directions, try new things, and step outside of our comfort zones. We tiptoed into it very cautiously and self-consciously, but came out on the other side with confidence, passion, and purpose.

Our Investigation phase can be divided into four areas:

1. Learn
2. Motivate
3. Experiment
4. Challenge

The purpose of this entire phase is to rekindle your curiosity, find your unique joys and passions, and then have the courage to follow through with them. It's time to investigate who you are truly meant to be. It's time to feel alive again.

1. Learn

As promised, this is going to start out easy. Jake and I had extremely low self-esteem, so our first step was to start learning within the safety of our own home. After you start gaining knowledge and experience on your own, it will be easier to branch out and find others doing the same thing.

Be brave and reignite your brain with the following steps.

Prioritize Personal Growth

When we started setting aside time every day to learn, it was empowering. We were affirming our self-worth over work and chores that never ran out. For so many years, we had allowed our to-do list to rule our lives. There was always "work" to do that was more important than reading a book for fifteen minutes or going to a class on Wednesday evenings.

We used our thirst for knowledge as fuel to start standing up for ourselves and setting boundaries with work schedules and responsibilities. The message we sent to ourselves was that we were important. Not only were we gaining amazing knowledge in the subjects we were interested in, but we were raising our self-respect and gaining confidence along the way.

For some reason, children are expected to spend the first twenty years of their lives dedicated to learning. Then we switch it off completely and join the workforce. But it should never be switched off. We should prioritize learning and personal growth for our entire lives. It is very important to acknowledge that personal growth is worthy of your time, and that you are worthy of personal growth.

Set aside time every day to learn, even if it's just ten to fifteen minutes. Or set aside time once a week to attend a class. Then prioritize it over all your chores!

Enrich Your Mind with Books

After college, I stopped reading. I had other hobbies like art, video games, and outdoor activities, but I completely lost my habit of reading. Luckily, a few years ago, audiobooks and a long commute to work changed that for me. I started listening to fiction books and slowly worked my way into non-fiction and personal development. The more I listened, the more I craved.

Then I realized that some of these books were better if I had them in my hands. I could read the physical words, reread the pages that meant more to me, and highlight the parts that I wanted to remember and reference. Reading and listening to books helped me learn new things every day, and I was hooked. Now I can't go anywhere without a book in my hand. I even bought a small backpack to replace my purse so I can always carry a book when leaving my house.

Whether you consider yourself a reader or not, start reading or listening to books. Go to your local library and try a few, or buy the books you want to highlight and reference. If you are a slow reader like me, start with a few pages per day and don't stress over finishing a book that isn't interesting. There is a wide variety of books out there and the right ones will find you. Here is a very short list of some of the books we started with and inspired us the most, but they led to *so many more.*

Coaching: *Super Coach* by Michael Neill
Self-Help: *You are a Badass* by Jen Sincero
Finding Yourself: *Eat Pray Love* by Elizabeth Gilbert
Awareness: *The Power of Now* by Eckhart Tolle
Productivity: *Who Not How* by Dan Sullivan
Wealth: *Rich Dad Poor Dad* by Robert T. Kiyosaki

You can find a full list of our favorite books on our website: brilliantlifejourney.com/resources/must-reads

Expand Your World with Podcasts

I was mowing the lawn early in this journey when Jake recommended that I listen to a podcast to pass the time, specifically *The School of Greatness* with Lewis Howes. I had never listened to podcasts before, but I had to wear ear protection anyway, so I decided to give it a try.

I was instantly transported away from my chores and into a new world. All the things that I wanted to learn about were being handed to me in an entertaining and easy way. I binge-listened to as many episodes as I could fit into my schedule. Each one featured a different guest, which led me to other podcasts and books, which led to still other podcasts and books. Now my podcast list is too long to ever get through. I love listening to them whenever possible.

Find a personal development podcast that intrigues you and start listening. Let this lead you to other podcasts, people, or books that intrigue you. Use downtime when driving or doing chores to listen and learn.

Sign up for Seminars, Workshops, and Classes

When I was ready to get back into pottery again, I found a Community Ed beginner-level pottery class. I was far from a beginner, but it had been a few years, and I wanted to reintroduce myself in an easy way.

I regained my confidence with some practice, built on my knowledge, and got to know other people who enjoyed creating art. This class eventually led me to being hired by a local pottery shop. I would have never had the confidence to apply without that baby step.

This is not meant to be a challenge or something scary. Find a class or a group setting that allows you to learn about something you already enjoy while connecting you with others who feel the same way. The easiest way to join is finding a subject matter you already have some experience or knowledge in. And feel free to pretend that you are a beginner!

2. Motivate

Like everyone, our motivation comes in waves. Jake and I continue to go through different seasons of life that either energize or drain us. Some waves come and go in an instant, others last for years. We can't always control the external life situations that feel defeating or depleting. In order to get through them and to build our own internal motivation, we have a few habits and activities that we rely on.

Listen to Energizing Music

Every time we get into the car, my daughter Maya asks, "Can you turn on Imagine Dragons?" It has turned into her catchphrase. We smile or laugh because we know it's coming, but then we always follow her instructions. They're the only musical group that our entire family consistently agrees on. No matter our individual or combined moods, the music seems to lift us up. The more we listen to their music, the better we feel, and the deeper the meanings are for us. We have realized that the music we listen to affects our mood, energy levels, thought patterns, relationships, and surrounding atmosphere.

Be very intentional about the music you listen to. Choose positive, meaningful lyrics and melodies that make you feel good. It will change your mood and your day.

Create Mantras, Affirmations & Intentions

When we were still living in rural Minnesota, my local elementary school approached me and asked if I could help them paint some murals based on the book *The 7 Mindsets to Live Your Ultimate Life* by Scott Shickler and Jeff Waller. This was before I had much experience or interest in personal development, but I took the task seriously. I read the book and designed seven murals to embody the meanings. I volunteered one day a week for the next year painting the inspirational murals throughout the school. The hallways were transformed from cold white to colorful and joyful.

I painted the murals to give back to my kids' school and make it a better place for students to learn. What I didn't expect was how the messages I was designing and painting seeped their way into my brain. And the more they repeated in my mind, the more I believed in them. This was my first experience with mantras and affirmations.

Now I create my own mantras, affirmations, and daily intentions. Some are daily reminders on my phone, some I read outloud, some I write in a journal, and some I hang up around my house. They express the ways that I want to show up in the world and the ways that I want to feel, and they are usually something that I struggle to believe. The more I repeat them, the more I accept and live into them.

Set a daily reminder on your phone with a mantra or affirmation that you read every day—out loud if possible. It should be in the present tense and positive, even if you don't believe it yet. *Especially* if you don't believe it yet. If there is something that you struggle with, flip it around and say the opposite. Search online for options if you need some inspiration.

Give Oracle Cards a Try

Okay, okay, I know what some of you are thinking. *What is with this woo-woo, fortune-telling nonsense?* I once thought the same thing. They seemed silly, strange, and a little scary, but we have come to find out they are the exact opposite.

Most decks of oracle cards have inspirational messages, and you can choose a card to help encourage your thoughts or actions. The cards spark new perspectives, empowering attitudes, and develop greater meaning behind the events in your life. We have a few different decks at home, and we like to choose one in the morning to help us set a daily intention. They can be used for any time frame or life question that you are dealing with. The messages are a way to help guide your mind and mood into a better place. Somehow the cards we pick at random always resonate with what is going on in our lives.

If you are intrigued and feel brave, buy a deck of oracle cards (also called affirmation cards or mantra cards). They usually come with a small book of optional instructions and the detailed meaning of each card. Use the positive messages to inspire and guide you.

Find Your Flow State

I have always been a creator. It doesn't matter what the art or craft is, I am happy to be making something with my hands. Time seems to slip by as I fall into my creative flow. I forget about eating, to-do lists, and all the things I normally worry about. It has been one of my greatest gifts, and I know it held me together during our toughest years and throughout my entire life.

If you have hobbies or activities that you enjoy, make sure to find time to do them. They don't have to be productive or purposeful. Simply creating the flow state in your brain and cultivating joy is the best reason possible.

Go To Your Happy Place

When we go on vacation, Jake turns into a different person. He relaxes, lightens up, and feels better. When we first started witnessing this phenomenon, it was a small glimpse back to the real Jake deep down. It was his true self shining through all the layers of anxiety and depression. And it was so discouraging when he sank back under those layers when we returned home. Just knowing that he was in there somewhere gave us hope to dig him out.

We did everything we could to bring him back, and he showed up more and more often. We intentionally went places that would light up his soul such as state parks, lakes, bowling alleys, friends' houses, and riding his motorcycle. Jake continues to struggle with stress, but physically moving to some of these locations is instant therapy.

Start noticing how you feel before, during, and after you spend time somewhere. If it lights you up, then prioritize those places and schedule more time where you feel your best. Spending as much time as you can in these places will build up positive energy to draw upon when you need it.

Follow Inspiring People

I once took an optional yoga class at an out-of-state conference. The instructor captivated me. Before leaving town, Jake and I traveled to her private studio and took a pilates class. Jake was as impressed with her as I was. After the class, we found out that she offered online classes, and I signed up. Everything about Julie inspired me, and I wanted to learn as much as possible. We started signing up for all her online training opportunities and eventually hired her to be our Life Coach. It is because of her that we were able to shift our lives in a healthy direction. I am so grateful for the amazing influence Julie has had on our lives.

Get curious about how you feel before and after you spend time with specific people. Prioritize those who motivate and energize you.

3. Experiment

One of the greatest gifts of our lives was having children. We have two girls who at the time of writing this book are ages ten and twelve. They bring joy, laughter, energy, and love into our house. I believe that they are teaching us more than we are teaching them. They encourage us to act silly, be playful, have fun, question rules, try new things, and keep learning. Life doesn't have to be so serious.

Remember Childhood Joy

When I was a kid, I loved organizing and performing in talent shows for my neighborhood and at school. I was proud to be part of it all—theater, band, choir, gymnastics routines, and sometimes all of them combined into one spectacular show. But I no longer had time for things like that during college, and then I lost it completely.

It wasn't until my mid-thirties when a couple of community members were trying to organize an arts board that I fell back into it. I barely had the courage to show up for the first few meetings, but slowly gained confidence with each experience. I started volunteering my summers to help with the community musical. The first year I quietly helped backstage, but as each year passed, I took on bigger responsibilities. From the pit orchestra to chief scenic painter, to a small on-stage role, to the leading role of Maria in *The Sound of Music*. The more involved I got, the more joy I found, and it spilled over into the other parts of my life.

Think back to your childhood and make a list of all the things that brought you joy: hobbies, activities, games, foods, places, etc. Commit to reigniting the spark of each one of those items on your list. You don't have to go all-in, just a small step is enough. Revel in the nostalgia of that joy and then see how far you want to follow it. Allow it to be fun and pretend you are a kid again.

Spark Your Interest

When we were in full-time farming mode, Jake needed a new way to level up his career. Someone reached out and recommended that he apply for a two-year leadership program called Minnesota Agriculture and Rural Leadership (MARL). He was excited to learn more within his career field and improve his leadership skills. It offered monthly seminars and networking around the state, a group trip to Washington, D.C., and a two-week international tour. The experience, knowledge, personal growth, confidence, and friends that Jake received from this program were priceless.

Get involved and join a group of people who share your interests. Find an organization, a volunteer opportunity, or a community group. Start by asking at your local library, your chamber of commerce, or a local school. The more you put yourself out there, the more opportunities will find you.

Try Something New

After we exhausted our options with classes and organizations that fit within our interests, we started wondering about the opportunities that were completely outside of our wheelhouse. The Rural Electric Board was looking for a new director in our district. I had zero experience with the electrical industry and the geographical footprint was an area we rarely traveled. By this time in my life, though, I had the courage and curiosity to give it a try. I got to meet new people, travel to new places, and gain a huge amount of knowledge and appreciation for the electricity that I had taken for granted my entire life.

Find an opportunity that feels completely out of character for you or something you know nothing about. Then be willing to try it. Don't worry about looking like a beginner or embarrassing yourself. Other people will actually find joy in helping you learn if you have a good attitude.

Create Data Points

The potter's wheel is one of the great loves of my life, but it has been a struggle to incorporate it into a career. After taking college courses and community classes in ceramics, I landed my first job as a production potter. Eventually, the hours and the monotony depleted me, so I started my own pottery business.

I tried functional pieces, but it was too repetitive. I tried statement pieces, but they were too difficult to sell. I tried creating a YouTube channel, but the technology and social media posts drained my time and energy. I tried giving pottery lessons, but couldn't find enough clients. I continued to pivot in new directions but couldn't make it work out. These have all been data points in my life that I have learned from. They eventually added up to the conclusion that I had to change course. I loved the potter's wheel for its therapeutic influence in my life, but I couldn't find a way for it to bring enough value to others so the career felt empty.

Not everything turns out the way we want or expect. Be flexible and learn from what works and what doesn't. There is no sunken cost to worry about when the data points push you in the right direction. The only thing you should avoid is continuing down the wrong path.

Advance Your Interests

Yoga fascinates me. The more I learn about it, the more I love it. A few years ago, I started with videos at home, then an online subscription, then online classes, then in-person classes, then week-long yoga retreats.

Finally, I began a Yoga Teacher Training course so I could improve my knowledge and practice even further, and potentially teach others. It was a slow and steady progression that grew into a very important part of my life.

If there is something in your life that intrigues you, start leaning into all the ways you can incorporate it into your life. Then investigate ways you can take it to another level. Most likely, you won't have to look too hard because the next step will naturally find you.

Explore Your Spirituality

When I was about seven years old, my dad had his own midlife awakening. He left his manager position at Del Monte to become a Lutheran minister. Our family moved to another state so he could attend a theological seminary for four years, and then he was called to serve at a church in rural Minnesota.

Since then, I have been a "preacher's kid," and people have always assumed that I am religious. In fact, it would be very taboo to say otherwise. I was not given a choice of which religion resonated with me nor offered the chance to explore spirituality. It caused an internal wall to be built up, and I secretly disregarded all religion.

That is, until we had the opportunity to hear Reverend Dr. Michael Beckwith speak in person. It happened to be at a conference that had nothing to do with religion. It caught Jake and me off guard, and it was the perfect moment for his message to sink in. The way he explained spirituality connected with me so deeply that the world started making sense. We now follow Rev. Beckwith online, and we love watching his Sunday services which are live-streamed from the Agape International Spiritual Center. We even attended one of the Sunday services in person when we were in Los Angeles.

Exploring religion and spirituality can be very challenging. It is an extremely difficult subject in the Midwest, and people can be deeply offended or judgmental. If you were raised in a religion that resonates with you, then you are lucky to have that strong spiritual balance in your life. However, if you struggle to understand or accept what has been handed to you, I encourage you to have an open mind.

Start learning about all religions, spiritual leaders, and communities. Something or someone out there can help you make sense of your life and feel connected.

4. Challenge

I hope you are feeling the momentum of all the small, easy steps. I hope you are feeling inspired to learn and grow, and are feeling proud of your unique set of skills and interests. Now, it's time to start challenging yourself.

Find Your Limiting Beliefs

"I'm not a runner," Jake said for almost forty years of his life. He wholeheartedly believed the thought and the identity that accompanied it. But after challenging this belief and putting in some work, he now runs almost every morning. And he actually enjoys it. He even ran a marathon for the first time!

The two of us are filled with limiting beliefs that we continue to uncover. One of our most persistent is, "I'm not good enough." It holds us back from doing so many things.

What are your reasons or excuses for not following through on your desires? What are you constantly telling yourself that you can't do? Those are your limiting beliefs. Now, add the word "yet" to the end of all of them. Such as "I'm not a runner, yet" and "I'm not good enough, yet." Whatever reason or excuse you have, acknowledge your true potential to change with that small word.

Question the Norms

I grew up in the age of sugary breakfast cereal. It was the norm for kids to eat every day, and it's still a common breakfast staple. I let my own kids eat Lucky Charms for many years. But what makes this a breakfast food? And what about Pop-Tarts, muffins, donuts, and pancakes? Why do we eat these foods first thing in the morning?

I started asking questions, looking at ingredients, and wondering what foods would be best to start my day. I realized that I felt awful when I ate sweetened foods right away in the morning, and it threw off my eating habits the rest of the day. I would swing from sugar rush to sugar crash all day long.

Are you making decisions that are right for you? Or are you allowing society to tell you how to live? Question and be curious about everything that you do. Make sure you are aware of all the decisions you make in your life, how they are affecting you, and whether they align with your values.

Step Out of Your Comfort Zone

Our family went to a BMX bike park one night, just to ride the course for fun with our regular street bicycles. A dad and his son were there with their racing bikes and gear. We struck up a conversation, and after a few minutes, he offered us his racing bike to try on the course.

Jake excitedly accepted the offer and rode around the course. I was super intimidated and immediately said no. But as I watched, I could feel regret seeping into my brain. Normally I would have brushed it off and forgotten about it. But I started questioning myself. Why was I holding myself back? Why would I want to regret saying no to this opportunity? So I took a deep breath and said okay. I was terrified. I was awkward. I thought I was going to embarrass myself. But I didn't. And it turned out to be fun.

Do something that makes you feel intimidated, scared, awkward, or uncomfortable. If you usually hold back when others step up, then try to join in whenever possible. Say yes instead of saying no, and take advantage of those opportunities.

Dare to Fail

During one of our last years on the farm, Jake was ready to challenge himself in new ways. The position for County Commissioner opened up, and it was something he had been thinking about for a while. Running for public office was intimidating and daunting. He had to be willing to answer difficult questions, attend public events, and face community conflicts and scrutiny. The race itself sounded like a fun challenge whether or not he won the seat.

As fate would have it, Jake lost with a very respectable 42 percent of the votes. Losing the race was still painful, but he is grateful for the experience and would not change a thing.

Be willing to try, whether or not you might fail. If there is an opportunity that you don't feel ready for, chances are, it is there because you *are* ready. Just let go and get out of your own way. Learn from the experience and don't worry about the outcome.

Follow Your White Rabbit

As I write this book, Jake and I are currently following one of our own white rabbits, and it is the scariest and most exhilarating white rabbit that has eluded us for over a decade.

We are in the process of moving our family to Costa Rica. It is surreal to even see those physical words in a sentence together. I would have never dreamed this was possible six months ago, and it would have sounded absolutely insane a few years ago.

But we know deep down that this is the path to our highest purpose because it's the path that makes us feel *alive*. It sparks hope, joy, curiosity, adventure, passion, growth, and yes, even fear. But we finally have the courage and feel worthy enough to chase our dreams. Not in ten years, but today.

And when we ask ourselves the three questions about our new home in Costa Rica, it brings a smile to our faces.

* Do you like to breathe the air? Yes
* Do you like the climate? Yes
* Is there clean water? Yes

Our white rabbit of curiosity, joy, and adventure had been lost from view for so long that we didn't even remember it existed. But we had followed it once before. Almost twenty years ago, we had the same fire burning within us, and it inspired us to join the Peace Corps and live abroad. It was one of the happiest times of our lives. We felt light and free. But it was also terrifying and challenging. It pushed us out of our comfort zones and forced us to grow. We felt alive.

Our white rabbit is finally in view again. It is extremely overwhelming and scary. There are people who challenge our decisions and make us question our path. We don't know what is waiting for us down the rabbit hole that we are about to jump into. Not everything will turn out the way we expect. **But the only thing more terrifying than following this adventuresome white rabbit is not following it, and then regretting it for the rest of our lives.**

Not all white rabbits are this wild, and they certainly won't start by jumping out of the country. Orient yourself in the right direction so that you can find your own white rabbit. Then start following it. Follow your curiosity, your joy, your intuition, and your unique calling in this world. Everyone's journey is different and perfect for them. If you can find your white rabbit, it will lead you exactly where you need to go.

PHASE 3
Activate

CHAPTER 6

Activate

Now, it's time to *go*. It's time to *activate*. It's time to *ignite* your inner fire and *unleash* the chains. This is the chapter where we get *serious*. This is the chapter where you turn into a *badass*. And what better place to start than *Sesame Street*?

Like most kids growing up in the Midwest, we were taught all the things we should do. We could rattle them off without thinking: go to school, do your homework, get outside, eat healthy food, exercise, go to bed on time, and so on. When you stop to think about it, they aren't that complicated. They are the basic building blocks of our life. We learned them from parents, caregivers, teachers, and even TV shows.

But then we turned into serious, complicated adults. The building blocks of life were no longer important. Work, responsibilities, and chores became our life. We forgot about the basics. We focused on all the wrong things and our foundation began to crumble. Then our serious, complicated adult lives could not be supported.

Everything suffered.

So let's pretend we are kids again, and that life isn't serious and complicated. Let's set our egos aside, get back to the basics, and strengthen our foundation. Let's pretend that learning and taking care of ourselves are the most important things.

Sesame Street—No Better Place to Start

When you were young, did you ever watch the show *Sesame Street*? Just in case you missed out, it's an educational television show for kids about an urban neighborhood filled with a diverse set of colorful characters. They taught me a range of simple concepts like learning numbers and letters, social skills, life skills, and problem-solving.

Each monster puppet had its own strengths, weaknesses, and challenges to overcome. Together they created a well-rounded, functioning community that learned and grew together. I loved watching *Sesame Street*, and I must have absorbed the lessons at a very deep level because they are starting to reemerge as I peel back the layers of my life.

If you think about it, each of the *Sesame Street* characters can embody a different part of ourselves—a different building block of our life. They all need attention; they all need to learn and grow, and each of them is a very important part of the system. When you focus on strengthening that foundational system, everything in your life improves.

There are seven monsters that stand out to me, each with their own unique life lessons to teach:

1. Oscar the Grouch: Master the Mindset
2. Big Bird: Small Habits
3. Bert & Ernie: Routines & Rewards
4. Cookie Monster: Food Monster!

5. Count von Count: Fun with Friends
6. Grover: Relax
7. Elmo: Love

Maybe that kids' show is more significant than we give it credit for. As adults, we need help with all the same things, perhaps even more so because our egos resist. So do your best to let go, have an open mind, and work on things that may seem a bit elementary. Let's return to your childhood and strengthen your foundation at a very basic level. Imagine each of the *Sesame Street* monsters as a part of your life and as a piece of you.

1. Oscar the Grouch: Master the Mindset

Oscar the Grouch is an obvious place to start. Even if you've never seen the show, you can easily imagine his negative attitude. He is a curmudgeon who is always grumpy, irritated, and easily provoked. Oscar has grubby green fur and purposely surrounds himself with filth, which only adds to his sour personality.

Oscar is the perfect example of what *not* to do. He resides in the same neighborhood as the other characters, and yet he experiences life very differently. All the negative thoughts in his head make him feel angry. But the problem is not the neighborhood that surrounds him— the problem is him. The way he chooses to live and the perspective he chooses to have make everything more grueling. He is perpetually stuck in a bad mood and literally stuck living in a garbage can while all the other monsters move happily and freely around the neighborhood.

As an adult, it's easy to turn into a curmudgeon. We get upset and allow it to distort our perspective and justify our actions. Then those unhelpful choices bring us down even further. We are creating our own misery.

We can't control the external world, but we can control how we respond and how we show up. Shift away from your own inner grouch and master your mindset with the following action steps.

Focus on the Positives

I used to think that emotions were just something that happened to me as a result of my situation. I assumed they were a natural reaction to the external world. My emotions were other people's fault, not my own.

But that's not the case.

No one has access to your mind. Your thoughts are completely up to you. And it's the thoughts in your head that create the feelings in your body. So when I began to find the silver lining or to focus on the bright side of every situation, I felt better. When I felt better, then even more good things came into view. Even failures were an opportunity to learn and grow.

Focus on the positives so that you feel more positive. Empower yourself by focusing on what you do want instead of what you don't want.

Express Gratitude

When our kids are stuck in a really bad mood, we make them tell us three things they are grateful for. At first, it makes them even angrier, and they stare us down with the look of death. But eventually, after realizing that we won't back down or leave them alone until they do it, they come up with three things.

Sometimes they are purposely tiny or ridiculous. Sometimes they end up being beautiful and inspiring. Sometimes it takes a really, really long time. But no matter what they come up with, it changes their attitude *every time*.

It truly works.

Expressing gratitude is one of the simplest ways to change your mood, but it can be hard if you are stuck in a negative spiral. It is a skill that needs practice, and it's a habit that we need to intentionally cultivate in our daily lives.

When you are stuck in a bad mood, find at least three things to be grateful for. Even if you don't want to, do it anyway. Also, you don't have to wait until you are in a bad mood! Schedule a time every day to create a quick gratitude list. Then take it up a notch and express gratitude to others.

Clean Up Your Space

Our environment has a very big impact on us and it's a reflection of who we are. The garbage can that Oscar calls home adds to his bad mood and clearly shows his personality and values. When my house is cluttered and messy, it affects how I feel. My mind feels cluttered and messy, and I feel frazzled and crabby. But when my house is clean and organized, I feel so much better. I can think clearly, I feel motivated, I have the space to be creative, and I can relax with my family.

As a mom, I sometimes have to put my foot down and set clear expectations and boundaries about household duties. It's really tough since we all have very different standards of cleanliness. So I have to choose: do I just clean it up myself and move on, or do I insist that they share the workload? The second option is usually more work for me in the moment; not only is there whining, but I have to spend time showing them how and reinforcing progress. In the long run, it does pay off when they can clean up after themselves, organize, take good care of their home, and feel proud of their environment.

Treat your outer world the way you want to feel in your inner world. Clean. Organize. Decorate. Paint. If you share a living space with others, including kids, then it's crucial that everyone learns to clean up after themselves and share the responsibility. Create a chore schedule and set rules along with rewards.

Clean Up Yourself

My hairstylist, Jen, told me that there is a noticeable shift in a person's behavior after their haircut. She once had some rowdy young daycare boys with hair as wild as their personalities. They got into trouble and were not kind to others. After a fresh haircut, they saw themselves differently and their behavior improved. They were more respectful and didn't need time-outs anymore. Jen also sees a beautiful transformation in her older clients who have Alzheimer's or dementia. Even if they can't talk, they seem much happier afterward. Their caregivers have even told her how much they perk up.

Our physical appearance has a big impact on how we feel and act. We internalize the judgments that we have about ourselves and what we see in the mirror. When I stay in my pajamas all day long and don't brush my hair or teeth, I feel lazy and grubby. When I shower and get dressed in a nice outfit, I feel energized and productive. When I get my hair cut, I feel more confident and I have a fresh outlook.

Take good care of yourself. Practice good hygiene, groom yourself, and dress for the way you want to feel. It will make a huge difference in your mood, your confidence, and the way you show up in the world.

Fix Your Posture

If you walk down the street and observe people's posture, you can make a pretty good guess about their mindset and mood. The way we carry ourselves is a reflection of our thoughts and feelings. On the flip side, our thoughts and feelings can be affected by how we carry ourselves.

We can actually change the way we feel simply by changing our posture. Our body language is a method of communication. We show others and ourselves how we are feeling.

Start noticing your posture throughout the day. If you are slumped over, feel the difference when you pull your shoulders back. If your head and eyes are down, lift up through the crown of your head and look straight in front of you. If your arms are crossed, relax them down by your sides or place your hands on your hips. Feel the difference in your mindset and mood when you stand tall or hold yourself in an empowering posture.

2. Big Bird: Small Habits

Big Bird is an eight-foot-tall, bright yellow canary, and his presence is unmatched. His willingness to help, learn, and focus on simple life lessons makes him larger-than-life—physically, mentally, and emotionally. Nothing is too small or insignificant for him to work on. To me, he symbolizes the importance of having the minutiae of daily life figured out and the exponential growth that it creates within us.

We are the sum of our daily decisions and habits. Every decision matters, no matter how small. And those decisions build our habits. They either lead us toward the person we want to become or away from it. In his book, *Atomic Habits*, James Clear explains how small changes to daily habits affect the trajectory of our lives. He encourages people to focus on getting 1 percent better every day, and his message has inspired both Jake and me to stay the course. One step in a better direction will add up over time to produce astonishing results. The longer you stick to your habits and build on them, the bigger the results will become.

Channel your inner Big Bird by creating the following habits.

Sleep

When our kids were young, we were caught in a sleep-deprived trap. Every evening, we would tuck our toddlers into their beds and then celebrate the win by staying up late to enjoy a few hours by ourselves. Morning always came too quickly, and feeling tired was the norm. Weekends were amplified when we stayed up even later drinking and hanging out with friends. We would try to sleep in the next morning, but the kids would wake up and the day would start.

We were grumpy and exhausted, and it created a negative domino effect with all the other choices and habits in our lives. It took us years to learn a better way. Now, we go to bed at the same time as our kids (sometimes even before them). We still get a few hours to ourselves, but it's in the early morning. We get up by 5 a.m. and love it. Instead of feeling awful every morning, we feel amazing! Those early morning hours are crucial, and we will never go back.

Go to bed early, and get up early. Try 5 a.m. if you can! Set a schedule and stick to it seven days a week. That's right—not just on weekdays, but on weekends too.

Hydrate

When I was growing up, my mom would tell us to drink water for every ailment. This was before carrying around a water bottle was cool, and before the benefits of choosing water over soda or juice was well-known. She was way ahead of her time. No matter what we complained about, it was her solution. We would usually groan because it wasn't the answer we wanted to hear. Luckily she didn't back down because it hammered in an extraordinary water-drinking habit.

As an adult, I fully appreciate all the health benefits of staying hydrated. The first thing we do when we wake up is drink water. Correction—the first thing we do is a trip to the bathroom, but *then* we drink at least twenty ounces of water. It rehydrates our bodies after sleeping for eight hours and flushes out all the waste that our organs have been digesting and processing throughout the night. Then during the day, we try to drink about a gallon of water and limit all the other drinks and juices. The craziest thing is that when our water consumption is on track, we don't get sick. Water cleans out all our bodily systems and keeps us healthy.

Wake up and drink water. No exceptions. Track your water consumption throughout the day with a goal of drinking a gallon. Eliminate as many sweetened beverages as you can. If you find yourself not feeling well for any reason, drink an extra glass of water immediately.

Exercise

Jake always knew he should exercise, but never thought he could spare the time or energy. He resisted for many years, and his physical health deteriorated. Then one day he had an idea: just fifteen minutes. He decided that he would get on the treadmill for just fifteen minutes every morning. His mind was able to wrap around giving up such a small amount of time.

After a while, he gradually increased the amount of time and the intensity. He slowly built up his endurance, both physically and mentally. He started feeling all the benefits and it became a priority. Jake turned exercise into a daily habit starting from ground zero.

Create a habit of daily movement. Start very slowly, and commit to a time and activity that is sustainable. If you prefer variety, then rotate between a few activities. Start with whatever you can wrap your head around, then slowly increase. If you already exercise once a day, try twice a day! I know, it shocked me the first time I heard it, too.

Connect

After a few years of working on ourselves, we had enough courage to start talking to people our age. We got to know two other young families who were involved in many of the same activities. We timidly invited them to hang out and were super excited when they accepted. We became good friends, and our world lit up. We had joy, laughter, entertainment, heartfelt conversations, venting sessions, counseling, and therapy.

Nothing could replace the value those friends provided. They got us through the COVID lockdown, the family business breakup, and our midlife awakening. Although we no longer live close enough to spend regular time together, we will always feel a connection to them. We now understand the importance of spending time with others and finding friends who you truly vibe with.

Connect with friends and family on a regular basis. If you feel drawn to someone or find yourself crossing paths with the same people, it's probably for a very good reason. Invite them to hang out and develop a friendship. If in-person is not an option, then at least reach out online.

3. Bert & Ernie: Routines & Rewards

Bert and Ernie are a pair of puppets who overcome challenges together even though their personalities are quite different. Sometimes it creates a nice balance, but other times it causes serious problems. Unfortunately, they never seem to learn the repeating lesson: Ernie needs a routine. Bert wants to jump into the next activity, but Ernie needs rituals to ease himself into it.

In some of the most iconic skits, Ernie is supposed to fall asleep simply by closing his eyes. But it is never that easy. He struggles. He can't make himself fall asleep when his brain and body are not ready. Bert and Ernie end up going through a whole list of wind-down activities that eventually put Ernie to sleep. But then Bert has put so much extra effort into the tasks that he ends up feeling wide awake.

If Bert and Ernie could just automatically rely on those wind-down activities and create a calming routine, the stress of trying to fall asleep would disappear. Ernie wouldn't feel the pressure to instantly switch from wake mode to sleep mode. Bert wouldn't have to get so worked up helping him, or resentful for giving up on his own sleep schedule.

Routines and rituals aren't just for kids; they are important for all of us. And they make life so much easier! Let's learn from Bert and Ernie's struggles and try these.

Establish an Evening Routine

When our kids were very young, it was common knowledge that they needed to wind down before bed. You couldn't just set them in their crib and expect them to close their eyes. We would give them a warm bath, put their jammies on, snuggle, dim the lights, read books, and rock them until they were drowsy. Then they were very happy to lie down and fall asleep.

Why didn't we realize that we needed the same thing? We resisted by working late, watching screens, and doing chores late into the evening. Then we would hop into bed and wonder why our minds wouldn't switch off.

Now we have learned a better way. We have an evening routine that helps our bodies and brains wind down. An hour or two before bed, we stop eating, limit screens, sometimes take a shower or bath, put our jammies on, turn off bright or unnecessary lights, cuddle, and read. When my head hits the pillow, I can fall asleep within minutes.

Start an evening routine at least an hour before your optimal bedtime. Create a calm environment, dim the lights, and choose relaxing activities that will help you wind down and prepare for sleep.

Develop a Morning Routine

After diving into the healthy habit world, Jake came across a book called *The Miracle Morning* by Hal Elrod. It combines a wide variety of healthy daily habits that you complete in the early morning hours. We gave it a try.

We woke up early and committed the very beginning of the day to our wellness. Today we continue to rotate between different habits and routines depending on our season of life and our daily schedule. Our list of choices typically includes exercise, getting outdoors, reading, meditating, yoga, a cold shower, and eating a healthy breakfast. Once accomplished, we can tackle the day in a powerful and positive direction. Instead of allowing our moods to be controlled by the demanding and volatile external world, we focus inward and cultivate the energy that we want.

Start a morning routine of healthy, empowering activities. Wake up early so that you can focus on your well-being before you jump into work, chores, and caring for others. Choose the way you want to show up for the rest of your day.

Rely on Rituals

Rituals can be used at any time of day to get you into the right mindset. There are times when I don't feel like exercising. So instead of thinking about whether or not I want to, I focus on putting my exercise clothes on. Then I choose some uplifting music or a podcast, get myself out the door, walk, and do some stretching. After all these rituals, my motivation is replenished and I am excited to exercise. My body and brain are accustomed to this procedure, and there is very little protest once I get going.

Use rituals to lead you into a desired activity. Use the momentum to eliminate resistance and create motivation.

Reward Yourself

When I was first getting into my exercise habits, I used to reward myself for using the treadmill or elliptical by watching a movie or a show. It was the only time I allowed myself to watch tv, so it motivated me to move every day and for longer amounts of time. I also rewarded myself with new exercise clothes and shoes that I got to wear during my workouts. I combined as many perks as necessary to make exercising enjoyable.

Reward yourself by adding fun activities before, during, or after your new habit, or buy something that will encourage you to keep going. Be careful that the reward doesn't completely negate the health benefits.

4. Cookie Monster: Food Monster!

Cookie Monster is a friendly blue monster with big googly eyes who tries so hard to do the right thing. But the temptation of cookies always gets the best of him. He struggles to exhibit self-control, but the longer he resists the temptation, the harder it becomes. Eventually, he completely loses it and yells, "COOKIEEEE!!!!" Then he shovels cookies into his mouth by the handful, while his manners and the cookie pieces fly in every direction.

When I was a kid, I loved Cookie Monster. And of all the characters on Sesame Street, he sticks in my mind the most. It's probably because I relate to his intentions and struggles. I try to be positive and disciplined, but sugar messes with my mind. It blocks my fullness cues, and I can't stop. The more sugar I eat, the more I want. The funny Cookie Monster from my childhood is now a disturbing reminder of the power that sugar has over me.

Food is a very sensitive subject. People are easily triggered and offended. Even changing your diet or politely declining food can upset others. We aren't here to tell you how to eat, and we certainly don't have it all figured out. What we do know is that there is a very serious problem. The standard American diet is the cause of obesity, disease, and so many health problems. Start asking questions about the food you eat. Be intentional about what you actually want to digest. Food can either power your body or drain your energy.

Here is our best advice on how to avoid Cookie Monster's predicament.

Eat Clean

After I realized the control that sugar had on me, I was able to start taking steps to empower myself. First, I eliminated the obvious culprits from my kitchen like candy and desserts. If it wasn't within sight or reach, then the temptation was nearly eliminated. Then I started looking at food labels and realized that some of my favorite "healthy" foods were packed full of sugar too! I was shocked to realize that the majority of yogurt, granola bars, and sports drinks had a ton of sugar hidden inside. Even "sugar-free" labeled foods contained sweeteners like sucralose that were just as bad and even more sneaky.

After cutting back on processed foods, our taste buds began to change. Overly sweetened foods, desserts, and candy lost their flavor and the temptation lessened. Many didn't even seem like food anymore. Whole foods like fruits and vegetables started tasting delicious, and we felt better after eating them. Now when we cut open a fresh pineapple or melon, Jake always says "This tastes like candy."

Include as many whole foods as you can into your diet. Eliminate as many processed foods as possible. Your taste buds will slowly acclimate and appreciate the healthier options.

Problem Solve

I dealt with acne for the majority of my life. I started going to a dermatologist during middle school and spent years trying all the medications. Nothing worked. I blamed it on hormones and genetics.

I knew the problem was coming from the inside and no amount of topical treatments would fix it, although it didn't stop me from trying.

Fast forward through a lot of painful and awkward years of trying to hide my face.

A few years ago I went through some embarrassing digestive problems and started eliminating anything I could from my diet to find the culprit. Eventually I found out that lactose, gluten, and sugar were causing my issues. And when I cut them out of my diet, something amazing happened. Besides the much-needed solution for my digestive organs, it was the external results that shocked me. My face cleared up! It was a huge relief when I learned this about myself. I was empowered to make different food choices that made me feel better.

Become aware of the immediate effects, long-term effects, and side effects of all the different foods you eat. Even if you don't deal with any noticeable health issues, try eating in different ways and see if it changes how you feel. What works for someone else may not work for you, so stay curious and pay attention to your own body.

Track Your Consumption

Jake and I had gotten so off track with the amount of food we were eating, that we no longer knew when we were hungry or full. We used food for so many reasons, and it was never to fuel our bodies. I would eat when I was stressed out, excited, procrastinating, celebrating special occasions, and just because it happened to be in front of me.

We had no idea how much we were eating until we started logging our food. Jake found the Noom app, and we began to track how many calories we were consuming throughout the day. The amount was shocking. With that information, we were able to start understanding what being full actually felt like. We are slowly healing our brain-gut connection.

Find an app to log and track your food. We started with Noom, but I'm sure there are a lot of options out there. You don't have to log every day, just try to understand your eating habits and caloric intake to empower your future choices. Use it as a tool for mindful eating, but not a rigid set of rules or limits.

5. Count von Count: Fun with Friends

Count von Count is a kid's version of Dracula. From what I remember, the skit usually started with him brooding away in a lonely, dark castle. He played gloomy music on his pipe organ and felt depressed and lethargic. So what always turned him around? His favorite bats would fly in and he would start counting them. He would slowly pick up energy and speed. By the end, he was bouncing around, full of joy. All he had to do was engage in a simple activity with the "Batty Batty Bats" and it would turn his day around.

There are group activities in our lives that lift us up. For some people, it could actually involve counting. In fact, both my mom and my brother are math teachers. Helping students solve number problems brings them joy. I see them light up when my daughters ask them for math help.

This is not the case for everyone, including myself (which is why I send my kids to their grandma or uncle when they have questions about their homework). We all have our own unique interests and I realize that the following list may not resonate with everyone. If it doesn't, keep searching for your own group activities that lift you up when you are down.

Here are some ideas to help you find your own version of counting "Batty Batty Bats."

Join a Team

Jake surprised me one day and signed himself up for jiu-jitsu. For the next few months, he spent two nights a week learning a new skill and bonding with a new group of people. When the group would divide out and "roll" (fight one-on-one), it was always in a very friendly and supportive way. It energized him, and he came home in a positive mood. It gave him something to look forward to, a reason to get out of the house, and a connection with others.

Join a sports team or fitness group. It's not about the competition but the camaraderie.

Go to a Show

Jake and I break our curfew once in a while for a late-night concert or show. Even though we feel tired and groggy the next day, it is hard to pass up the opportunity. The energy of the crowd and the collective experience are unlike anything you can recreate alone in your own home. We always leave the event in a great mood.

Go to a live show and enjoy the group atmosphere. If you play an instrument, sing, or act, join a community group and share your love of music or theater from the stage.

Get a Pet

I felt painfully silenced during the last meeting of Rieke Farms. I was not supposed to be seen or heard. My jaw clenched, my throat tightened, and it gave me a pounding headache. After the online meeting concluded, it was all I could do to walk down the hall to my bedroom and lie down. Within minutes our cat came in, jumped up on the bed, and lay down right on top of my neck. It was the strangest experience.

I lay there wondering what in the world was going on. Then I fell asleep. The weight of her body and the warmth of her fur was exactly what I needed at that moment. It calmed me down and allowed my throat and jaw to relax. I am not sure if anything else could have had the same effect at that moment. Luckily, our cat had somehow pinpointed my pain and took the role of an intuitive healer.

Animals have a therapeutic presence. If you don't already have a pet, it's worth some serious consideration.

Attend a Yoga or Wellness Class

Okay, okay, I know I keep bringing up yoga.

It's because the more I learn and practice, the more I appreciate the wide variety of health benefits that a single activity offers. So when you add in the enjoyment of a group atmosphere, it makes the experience even more powerful! I can't say enough good things about group wellness classes like yoga.

Find a yoga studio or instructor in your area and give it a try! You could also try other types of wellness classes like Tai Chi, a sound bath, or a group meditation session. See if there are any studios nearby and explore the variety of activities that they offer.

Brave a Sauna & Cold Plunge

When I was a kid, I loved staying at hotels, mostly because there was usually a pool and a hot tub. We would go back and forth from the cold pool to the hot tub just for fun. Back and forth, back and forth, we basked in the quick temperature changes. It was a kid's version of a sauna and cold plunge before they were popular.

Today, sauna and cold plunges are gaining traction even in the Midwest. If you aren't sure what I am referring to, it's pretty much what it sounds like: you sit in a hot sauna for roughly ten minutes then submerge yourself in a very cold tub of water for 3–5 minutes, and then repeat.

The length of time and temperature can vary depending on where you go, but they all cause extreme temperature shifts for our bodies to regulate. Aside from the long-term health benefits of doing this regularly, many people feel instant results to their aches and pains, and a release from stress or anxiety. The temperature shocks your system and mindset into a new place.

Find a Sauna & Cold Plunge that is near you, and go for it! Some are stand-alone businesses, but you might also find them at day spas or wellness studios. It's certainly an option to do this on your own, but I highly recommend it with a group.

Try a Group Breathwork Session

When I was at the yoga retreat in Costa Rica, one of the most profound experiences I had was during a group breathwork session. I had never experienced anything like it before, but I was open-minded and ready for anything. We spaced ourselves out in a yoga studio and lay on our backs with mats and lots of blankets and pillows.

For about an hour, we breathed as deeply as possible through our mouths, listened to loud music, and let out a few primal screams together. (Think about it—when was the last time you screamed at the top of your lungs?) It allowed emotions to come up that I had been suppressing for years. I cried to the point of shaking. It was an emotional release that had been building up for a decade. I am not sure how or why this type of breathing can cause such powerful insights and emotional releases, but it transformed the way I saw myself and the world permanently. It was therapeutic and it was life-changing.

Everyone's experience with breathwork is unique. Jake tried an individual breathwork session but had a much different experience. By that time in our lives, he had already utilized many other methods for insight and emotional healing. His session brought calm clarity but not any unexpected emotions or epiphanies.

Look for options near you to try a group breathwork session. Make sure you feel comfortable and safe with the leaders and the location. Some practitioners offer individual sessions for people who want to try it on their own before participating in a group setting.

6. Grover: Relax

Grover is a wiry blue monster who tries hard to stay calm but always finds himself in hectic situations that test his resilience. He runs around in a frenzy, and you can see his stress levels rising as he tries to keep it together. He pushes himself to the limit, and it eventually gets the better of him. I remember most skits ending with him passing out from exhaustion.

Grover was so determined to keep up or solve the challenge that he wore himself out. He couldn't stop. We are all like this sometimes, or maybe *all the time*. We push ourselves too hard and refuse to take a break for our well-being. People assume that taking time out to recharge is selfish or lazy. But taking some time for yourself can change how you show up the rest of the day. It can actually improve your productivity; you get more done in a smaller amount of time when you clear away the mental clutter and relax the tension in your body. You will feel energized, motivated, positive, and increase your problem-solving creativity.

Gift yourself a break from the Grover-like pressure that is building up around you with some of these options.

Meditate Daily

One morning, my daughter Maya was triggered by something (that still has yet to be revealed) and sank into a pretty dark mood. When I tried to talk with her about the cause, she wanted nothing to do with me. All I got were shrugs and a cold shoulder. We insisted she go outside to get some fresh air, but that didn't seem to help either. Finally, she told me that she just wanted to be alone. So we let her be.

Maya went to her bedroom, and we didn't bother her again. She came out about an hour later and her mood was resolved. She hadn't slept, or played games, or read. She just lay in her blanket fort and decompressed. It was her way of getting quiet and going inward. It was her way of meditating.

Later that same day, Maya and Avery came up with a very interesting business venture. They sold guest passes and memberships for clients to spend quiet time in Maya's blanket fort. They called it "The Hidden Fort" with the tagline, "Hide away in a fort with no guilt and take a break from the craziness of life!"

I bought a bronze membership for five minutes per day and spent my first session lying in a quiet, comfy cocoon of blankets and pillows, letting my mind and muscles relax. It was like being in a meditation pod. I now completely understand why Maya had insisted on being alone and spending time in her fort.

Try meditating for 5–10 minutes every day. Set aside a specific time of day that you can commit to on a regular basis. I highly recommend trying a blanket fort as your private meditation pod.

Practice Yoga Regularly

Yep, this again. It's the cure-all for every situation. Kind of like how my mom recommends drinking water for every situation. I wonder if this is what my kids will remember about me?

Just a quick 5–10 minute yoga session will do wonders for mental stress or body tension. (You could also drink a glass of water.)

Take a Power Nap

When I get overwhelmed or stressed out, my head starts to pound. My brain feels like it has been overworked, overheated, and has swollen up to a point that my skull feels too small. It needs a serious break before it can function well again. When I feel this way, I am past the other options. The easiest way for me to hit the reset button is a quick power nap. Fifteen minutes usually works the best, but even just five minutes can help in a big way. It's not always a viable option to actually lie down and sleep, depending on where I am or what I am doing, but I can usually figure out a way to just close my eyes and rest my head against something for a few minutes.

Take a power nap to give your brain a much needed break. If that's not an option, find a way to rest your eyes and head for a few minutes.

Schedule an Appointment

When I schedule an appointment, I add it to my calendar, and there is no question whether or not I will go. The calendar effectively cuts me off from work, chores, and family responsibilities. It's built into my day, so I stop what I am doing and take a break.

And I never regret it.

When I take time out of my day to feel good, heal my body and mind, and work on myself, I show up better for those around me. Then I am in a better place to solve problems, I have more patience, and I connect better with those around me.

Schedule an appointment with a professional for your well-being. Try massage, acupuncture, Reiki Energy Healing, MBSR (Mind Body Spirit Release), ketamine therapy, or talk to a therapist, counselor, or mentor.

7. Elmo: Love

Elmo is a little red monster who has a heart of gold. He is not afraid to express his genuine love and appreciation for everyone around him, and the neighborhood loves him back. Elmo laughs and plays and cuddles, and he seems so light and happy as he bounces around the neighborhood with all his friends.

Elmo is the extreme opposite of Oscar the Grouch and is the perfect example of how we should live our lives. He radiates love and joy, and it reflects right back to him. When he expresses love to others, they always seem to reciprocate. It brings out the best in everyone, everything, and every situation.

Practice living with Elmo's simple yet profound outlook.

Show Love

I was recently in the Sky Lounge at the Atlanta airport while we were waiting for our next flight. There was a manager monitoring the area, and I couldn't help but stare at him, and even pointed him out to Jake. He was a young, handsome guy who was absolutely rockin' a sharp black suit and walked around like he owned the place.

I was super intimidated and felt pretty grubby in comparison. But for some reason, I wanted to tell him how great he looked. I finally worked up my courage after walking past him a number of times.

"Wow, you look *amazing* in that suit. It makes me want to dress better."

He immediately softened. I could feel the good energy being reciprocated back to me. Then he told me that it was actually his first day on the job! He said the compliment was exactly what he needed. And all it took was a little courage to compliment a stranger.

I realize this may not be the traditional definition of expressing love, but the genuine interaction really did open up a connection between us. I felt love and joy toward him and within myself after our quick conversation.

Be vulnerable, tell your family and friends how much you care about them, or compliment a stranger. The more love you give, the more love you will receive.

Love Yourself

All of the advice in this chapter has led up to this grand finale! In fact, I would argue that everything in this book has led us up to this. All the suggestions and advice we have given are methods to build your self-respect, your self-worth, and ultimately, your self-love.

When Jake and I were in the depths of our darkest days, our self-love scale had bottomed out at zero. We hated who we were, how we felt, and how we acted. The journey that turned our midlife crisis into a midlife awakening was actually a journey toward loving ourselves again.

We started listening to ourselves, living our truth, treating our bodies with care, and allowing our minds to expand. We started growing in numerous ways and building self-respect and confidence. And maybe there was always a hint of self-love hiding out beneath the loathing. Maybe that's what actually pulled us through. It is an ongoing process. The more we continue to grow and accept ourselves, the more we allow self-love to bubble to the surface and create peace in our lives.

Find a picture of yourself as a baby or toddler, or dig up a possession that you loved: a stuffed animal, toy, or blanket. Feel the joy, hope, and love that emanated from that little human. Remember your innocence, best intentions, and pure potential. That beautiful soul is still within you. Love yourself like you love your own child. Unconditionally.

Get Back to the Basics

The lessons of each of these monsters are important for kids to learn, and even more important for adults to remember. All of these inner monsters contribute to the foundation of our well-being. Unfortunately, we no longer have our parents, caregivers, or teachers to enforce the lessons.

It was easier when we were kids because we were held accountable by the adults in our lives. We may have rolled our eyes, grumbled, or protested, but we had to obey their rules. Learning, growing, and taking good care of ourselves was our job and we were expected to follow instructions, practice, and do it well. But even though we had to follow all those rules, we felt wild and free. Our bodies and brains were growing at a crazy speed. The world was full of hope and joy, and anything was possible.

How do we return to those feelings?

Start living like a kid again. Follow all the same basic rules of healthy living that you learned from *Sesame Street* when you were young. But now that we are adults, we have to cultivate self-discipline to take the place of authority figures. And it is *really difficult*. No one is going to make you go outside when you need fresh air. No one is going to sign you up for soccer and drive you to practice. No one is going to limit the amount of cookies you eat. No one is going to take away your phone and make you go to bed on time. You have to generate the discipline within and hold yourself accountable.

Former Navy Seal Jocko Willink often says, "Discipline equals freedom" and even has a book with the same title. It felt counterintuitive the first time I heard those words together. Discipline did not sound like freedom at all. It sounded like the exact opposite. It sounded like taking all the fun out of your life and making yourself do all the things that you hate.

But when Jake and I started creating self-discipline with healthy habits, there was a dynamic shift in our lives toward freedom. Our energy levels sky-rocketed, we could move with more ease, sports were more fun, small spaces like airplane seats were more comfortable, we started joining in activities that were once too intimidating, and we didn't hit that afternoon slump. We were free to do so many more things and enjoy our lives in so many more ways.

It turned out to be absolutely true: discipline *did* equal freedom. Our bodies were free from physical limitations, our minds were free from constant brain fog and stress, and we were free from our reliance on addictive substances. It was opening up new opportunities, new levels of momentum in our personal and professional lives. We were becoming fierce, creative, resilient, and unstoppable. Our inner fire was expanding, but more importantly, our freedom was expanding.

You can change your life. And you can start *at this very moment.*

You know what to do. Be your own parent. Discipline yourself. All those rules that we expect kids to follow are just as important for us as adults. Make good decisions no matter how small or trivial they seem.

Control your thoughts and emotions. Cultivate simple, healthy habits. Build and follow routines. Make food choices that empower you. Join fun group activities. Schedule regular time-outs to relax and recharge. Most of all, show kindness and love to everyone, especially yourself.

Rediscover what you have always known. Live the lessons that *Sesame Street* taught you and become the badass that you were meant to be.

PHASE 4
Eliminate

CHAPTER 7

Eliminate

June 2021: Confusion. Dread. Panic. Then ABSOLUTE FEAR.

The whole family was going to hate us, and there was nothing we could do. I was paralyzed with fear, and my life came to a screeching halt.

The reality was revealed at a difficult moment. I was working at a kid's theater camp for the summer. I was supposed to be walking into the auditorium ready to start the day, ready to lead a group of middle school students with fun activities. But I couldn't get out of my car, I couldn't face anyone, especially the kids who needed inspiration and support. I was supposed to be the strong one, but I was a wreck. The veil of our Matrix reality had been ripped away, and I didn't know who or what I could trust any longer.

"The farm isn't going to survive, and everyone's going to blame us. What can we do?" I whispered, tears streaming down my face. I sat frozen while the world was caving in.

I was on the phone with Jake when the future became crystal clear. "I don't know," Jake replied. And we sat in a dark silence.

We had started down the path of personal development and made enormous strides. We were finally using the tools and habits to unlock our minds and bodies. But the new clarity and confidence had unveiled a major storm headed right for us.

The farm wanted us to stay put, to continue business as usual, to fulfill our daily chores, and to stop questioning the future. But the transition plan was deeply flawed, and there was no way we could ever afford to buy the company. The family farm was going down a dangerous path.

We had worked with such loyalty and faith for the past decade. We had believed that eventually the farm would take care of us in return. But during that phone call, we realized it was impossible. If we kept going down this same road, it would lead to bankruptcy.

No.

We decided that we had to find a solution, a compromise, so that the family business and family legacy could continue. We resolved to figure it out. We had already put over a decade into this life. There was too much sunken cost for us to start over. Jake was turning forty that year, and there wasn't time to begin a new career and a new life. So we held on tight, more determined than ever to figure out a plan forward. We spent the next ten months of our lives trying to hold on to the family farm. It was painful. It was hard. There was resistance at every turn. We hired multiple professionals and specialists to try to figure it out. But the harder we tried to hold on, the harder it got. We felt completely powerless and trapped.

April 2022: Clarity. Peace. Stillness.
Then ABSOLUTE BLISS.

I sat calmly while the world was opening up.

I was on the phone with Jake when the future became crystal clear.

"I know," Jake replied. And we sat in a dazzling silence.

This was the phone call I made from the yoga retreat in Costa Rica. This was the moment we finally let go. Over the past ten months, the Universe had blocked us at every turn. We had tried every solution, every compromise that our team could come up with. But common ground was never found. And now, we were genuinely grateful. A weight was lifted off our shoulders when we realized that no amount of loyalty or hard work would save the family farm. The conflict freed us, and we did not have to accept a life of servitude to uphold the family legacy.

Jake and I let go of our plans. We let go of trying to control the outcome. We let go of our ownership in the family farm. We both knew, without any discussion, that it was the only way out. And it was the true beginning of our freedom. Feeling stuck for all those years had been one-hundred-percent self-inflicted. Our own resistance to the future had been holding us captive. We finally released the chains holding us down.

The future was now wide open. We could begin a brand new life. We could learn, grow, become better humans, find our true purpose, pursue a fulfilling life, and inspire others to do the same. We felt completely free.

Two Phone Calls. Two Opposite Outcomes. The Exact Same Situation.

The first call was filled with complete resistance and torment. We tried to control the situation and hold on tight. We were stuck.

The second call was filled with complete acceptance and peace. We had to trust ourselves and let go of everything. We were free.

The choice had always been there, but it took a long time to see it. For us, letting go would not have been possible without first activating our self-worth and self-love by increasing our physical, mental, emotional, and spiritual health. We had to start growing.

During our phases of Contemplate, Investigate, and Activate, we added so many positive things into our lives that the negative things no longer had space to thrive. We generated so much self-respect that we had the confidence to stand up for ourselves and question the artificial authority that kept us stuck. We created so much momentum and growth that we were able to let go of the toxic elements holding us back.

Don't Wait. Eliminate.

Eliminating something from your life can be much more challenging than adding. There is a grieving process that takes place when you realize you will never be the same person again. Sometimes you lose things that you didn't expect. Sometimes you have to let go of things that once brought you joy. It is always your choice whether you hold on to the old you and suffer, or let go and allow the new you to unfold.

You are meant to grow, but not everything or everyone is going to evolve with you. The more you resist, the harder your life will be. And when you are finally able to let go of everything holding

you back, you will find true freedom. You will wonder why you didn't do it a long time ago. And there is more good news! When you eliminate the parts of your life that are holding you back, it opens up space for even more new opportunities and growth.

Now that you have had a chance to add new thoughts, behaviors, activities, people, and places into your life, it's time to eliminate some that no longer serve you.

There are four areas of our Elimination phase that we want to focus on:

1. Detach From Unhealthy Behavior Patterns
2. Overcome Destructive Thought Patterns
3. Remove External Harm
4. Craft an Identity

Our goal is to get rid of everything that is holding you back from your full potential, and anything toxic to your soul.

Eliminate, and continue growing.

1. Detach From Unhealthy Behavior Patterns

You probably already know the behavior patterns in your life that are holding you back. It's up to you to step up and eliminate them. Use all your new healthy activities and habits from our Activate phase to fill up your life, disrupt the unhealthy elements, and then detach from them completely. Here are some places to start.

Eliminate Alcohol & Recreational Drugs

After both Jake and I prioritized healthy habits like sleep, exercise, and a healthy diet, alcohol no longer fit into our lifestyle. We no longer stayed up late—the hours that the majority of people drink. We stopped going to bars, breweries, and wineries. We spent our social time in healthier ways with fitness classes and wellness activities. Our downtime was filled with reading, learning, exercising, and nature.

Our previous drinking problem was barely in our awareness. And most importantly, we no longer identified ourselves as "drinkers" or "partiers." Instead, we filled up our lives with the habits we wanted, and drinking alcohol no longer fit our new values or identity.

Start focusing on healthy habits and behaviors, and the unhealthy ones may naturally fade away. Choose options that make you feel good in the long term over the ones you are going to regret tomorrow. If you truly want to upgrade your life, then don't allow toxins like alcohol or recreational drugs to slow you down.

Avoid Junk Food & Overeating

Jake and I have found a lot of ways to clean up our diet. We rarely buy junk food and do our best to limit restaurants. Societal and familial pressures to eat are one of our biggest challenges. Sometimes we find ourselves falling back into old eating patterns, especially when we return to our parents' houses or go out to eat with friends. It's a constant process of uncovering unhealthy habits and detaching from the triggers.

One of the easiest strategies I have to curb overeating is to stay hydrated. When I focus on drinking water throughout the day, I naturally eat less. I always carry a water bottle, and it gives me something to hold or to do when others are eating in front of me. Jake loves sparkling water for the same reason.

Make changes in your life that disrupt the eating patterns you want to avoid. Drink lots of water, carry a water bottle or healthy snacks, stop buying junk food, avoid restaurants or places where you lose self-control, and change up your daily routines.

Refrain from Mindless Scrolling & Screens

We used to watch TV every night, and the behavior pattern became a dependency. I didn't believe I could fall asleep without it blaring down on us in our bedroom. But all that changed when we committed to reading ten pages a day. Sometimes, we didn't have time to get our daily reading done until the evening. It started creeping into our normal TV time.

Instead of lying in bed watching TV, we would read. I would read until I was so tired that I couldn't keep my eyes open. I proved to myself that I didn't need the TV to fall asleep. Reading took over, and I was finally able to let go of a very unhealthy habit. Now I absolutely love to read, and I choose it over TV anytime—day or night.

Commit to reading every day, and use it to disrupt your normal screen time. Or commit to exercise or a family activity when you normally sit on the couch and rely on TV for entertainment.

Stop Frivolous Spending

Jake and I broke up for a summer during college, and I struggled to fill the void. That's when I found shopping. I would go to the mall and buy clothes, jewelry, and stuffed animals to cheer myself up. I felt good on the way home, but it never lasted. For many years, I used shopping as a coping mechanism when I was feeling hurt or sad.

It wasn't until we started using money in a better way that I got over this bad habit. Jake and I started reading books like *Rich Dad Poor Dad* by Robert Kiyosaki. We learned about investing money for the future and creating passive income. We had a greater purpose for our money, and I no longer wanted to spend it on frivolous things. We started investing in ourselves and in our future.

Find ways to invest your money that excite you, then say goodbye to wasting money.

2. Overcome Destructive Thought Patterns

Finding and releasing destructive thought patterns is a whole other beast. There seems to be no end to the amount of layers to uncover. Plus, you have to analyze your thoughts, by using your thoughts. It's a very tricky level of self awareness, and your ego will try to block you at every turn.

Below are three types of thoughts that held Jake and me captive for years. From our experience, they are the most common issues that keep people stuck. Start observing your own thoughts, find the patterns that are sabotaging your life, and let them go.

Break Free From the Victim Mindset

On my thirtieth birthday, I was living in a permanent victim mindset. I didn't believe I was in control of my life or emotions, and I always wanted my husband to take care of me. But instead of waiting around feeling sorry for myself, I should have taken responsibility and action. Instead of focusing on what other people were doing, or not doing, I should have been focusing on what I was doing. It took a long time for me to learn, but I am proud to say that I continue to make progress releasing the victim mindset and taking responsibility for my thoughts, feelings, and actions.

By my fortieth birthday, I learned to be my own hero and appreciate the people in my life so much more. I took decisive action and did not once feel sorry for myself. The victim mindset still creeps up on me once in a while, especially as a mom. Sometimes I get wrapped up in how other people are affecting me, instead of how I am affecting myself. It helps to remind myself that *I control my actions, and I control my time.*

Step up and be your own hero. If something is important to you, don't sit around and wait for someone else to do it, take some action and get it done. Be responsible for your thoughts, feelings, actions, and situation. No excuses, no apologies—just treat yourself the way you want to be treated and the world will follow suit.

Freeze Negative Thoughts

Jake used to be stuck in the habit of negative thinking. When challenges came up on the farm, he got upset. He thought that difficult situations caused the negativity in his life. And the negativity seemed to snowball. But getting upset only made the problem worse. His mind shut down to solutions and he pushed people away.

When Jake could see the situation for what it actually was—like a flat tire that needed his attention—there did not have to be any emotion attached to it whatsoever. He could just accept it, fix it, and move on. As he learned to move through challenges without negative thoughts, then the situations did not seem nearly as difficult. He could flow through his day with more ease and peace. The challenges and situations did not change, but his response changed how he felt.

Negative thoughts can spin out of control. Our bodies literally heat up from the energy. There is a reason we call someone a "hot head" or tell them to "cool off." Jake and I have begun to experience the truth in those sayings. When we get angry, frustrated, or overwhelmed, we can feel our internal temperature rising. Cooling off is our favorite way to snap ourselves out of it. The first opportunity we get, we take a quick cold shower and it works wonders. Depending on the severity of the negative thoughts, it sometimes takes a few.

If you find yourself spiraling down into negative thoughts, take a cool shower. If that's not possible, here are some alternatives: stand in front of a fan, wash your hands and face with cold water, step outside if you live in a cool climate, go for a swim if you live in a warm climate, or peel off an extra layer of clothing. Find a way to physically release the heat generated by your negative thoughts.

Defy Limiting Beliefs

Jake and I were getting ready to leave for the airport in about an hour. Everything was packed and ready to go. We knew that we would be spending a lot of hours cramped in a tiny space, so we decided to go for a short bike ride before leaving town. We were in good spirits, and we appreciated the fresh air and exercise. We only made it about a block before we stopped to talk to a neighbor. She was a retired lady who spent a lot of time on her garden and lawn. As we rolled up, she shot us a stern look and snapped, "What, ya got nothing to do???"

Apparently, going on a bike ride did not qualify as something to do. I recoiled in surprise and politely responded that we were on a bike ride. I certainly wasn't going to tell her that we were just about to leave for Costa Rica. If she thought that a bike ride was too frivolous, then traveling to Costa Rica to look for a new home was completely out of the question. We quickly said goodbye and went on our way, but her comment lingered.

Her sharp question had so many limiting beliefs packed inside it about work, time, exercise, and priorities. These were the exact limiting beliefs we were trying to free ourselves from. It was one of the reasons we wanted to move away from the Midwest. It is so easy to take on the limiting beliefs of the people who surround us. Traveling and living in different places has helped Jake and me gain new perspectives and challenge the old. If there had been any remaining doubt about moving to Costa Rica, this interaction successfully eliminated it all.

Travel outside of your communal bubble and be open to new ideas and new ways of living. You are not obligated to live the same life as anyone else. Start asking, "Why?" when something doesn't resonate with you. Then start asking, "Why not?" when new ideas pop into your head.

3. Remove External Harm

Identifying and eliminating elements in our lives that cause harm might sound obvious and simple, but in reality it's the opposite. It can be difficult to recognize and very complicated to remove. We always start out with the best of intentions, and it blinds us when reality slowly seeps in or when the situation morphs into disaster. Then we feel stuck with our jobs, relationships, or life situations. There could be a lot to unravel, along with some really hard conversions. Here are some areas in your life to evaluate.

End Toxic Situations

The farm didn't start out as a toxic situation for us. When we joined the family business, there was a lot to learn, and we were happy to soak it in and master the responsibilities. But we hit a ceiling of growth when we were expected to do the same things and the same chores, year after year. We weren't allowed to change the vision of the farm or to evolve the business in any meaningful way. Meanwhile, the transition of ownership slowed to a halt. We needed to keep growing ourselves and building our future, but this career was not transforming with us.

When we stayed in our place and prevented ourselves from growing, our souls protested with absolute agony. Depression set in, along with drinking, overeating, negativity, and so much more. All of these symptoms and coping mechanisms were trying to tell us something—*This is not a healthy environment for us. It's time to leave.*

If there are any situations in your life that prevent you from growing or becoming the person you want to be, get out of there as fast as you can. If you find yourself using unhealthy coping mechanisms in order to accept it, this is your body telling you to make a change.

Cut Ties with Toxic People

When our careers ended at the farm, our former business partners were still part of our extended family. And all the family dynamics and drama were even more difficult to navigate than the business negotiations. Everyone seemed to have a strong opinion, whether they had the correct information or not. Jake had to cut off contact with specific family members when it turned into verbal and written abuse. He stopped responding to phone calls and emails and blocked them on social media. We cut off contact as much as we could. We knew that we did not deserve the anger, hatred, or negativity that was directed at us. The more we disconnected from that energy, the better we felt.

If there are people in your life who direct anger, hatred, or resentment toward you, do everything possible to cut ties with them. Do not allow their negative energy to affect your life.

Leave Toxic Places

The farm itself is now a toxic place for us to be. When we step foot back on the property, painful memories and feelings surface. All the years that we spent and all the accusations we endured come flooding back. My throat closes up and my jaw gets tense. Moving to a nearby town helped distance us while Jake wrapped up the business side of things, but we knew that it was temporary. We knew that we had to get further away. Our goal was to at least leave the state. What we didn't know at the time was that we would gain ultimate space by leaving the country. The farther we get from the farm, the better we feel.

If there is a place that causes you physical tension, mental stress, or any kind of harm, do everything possible to distance yourself from it.

Minimize Painful Reminders

During my yoga retreat in Costa Rica, I participated in my first Full Moon Circle. It's a gathering during the full moon to reflect, set positive intentions and release what no longer serves you. We wrote down something we were ready to let go of on a small piece of paper.

Since Jake and I had just agreed that we were ready to let go of the farm, I wrote that down. The next morning, I realized that I had also released my last name, "Rieke." With some reflection, I knew that disassociating myself from that name could be really empowering, but logistically it would be a nightmare to legally change it. The solution came almost instantly.

I decided to pronounce the name differently. Instead of pronouncing it "Ricky," I now say, "Ray-key." Coincidentally, (or not?) it's the same pronunciation as the word "Reiki," which means Universal Life Force. It's a healthy way for me to detach from the painful memories every time I say my name out loud. It feels like an empowering, fresh start.

If there is something in your life that holds a negative or toxic attachment, find creative ways to change it.

4. Craft an Identity

Crafting a new identity involves setting rules for the person you want to be. And you have to be willing to let go of anything that doesn't fit within those parameters, or you will never be free to change.

Set Boundaries

I'm an introvert, so setting boundaries is really important for me. Now that I have more confidence and self awareness, I unapologetically say no when I don't want to do something. I tell my family when I need focus time to work. My cell phone is almost always on silent, and I let messages and emails wait until I am ready to read them. Sometimes I need physical distance from people to recharge, so I will shut my bedroom door or find another quiet place to decompress.

With my kids, I have to set boundaries with the amount of questions they can ask me, otherwise I don't have any time or mental space left for myself. Sometimes I have to tell them "Okay, you can only ask me three more questions today." Other times I find a quiet place where they cannot easily disturb me. And if it gets out of control, I blatantly say, "My brain is full, go ask your dad." If I don't set boundaries with them, I wind up losing my patience and feelings get hurt. Boundaries may seem harsh at first, but they help us treat everyone with kindness and respect.

Setting boundaries means protecting yourself, your time, and your energy. It allows you to determine the guidelines of how you live your life. It will probably be awkward when you tell someone no, but the clear limits will take emotion out of the equation. You may need to set different kinds of boundaries for different people. Communicate your boundaries to the people you love so that your relationships remain strong and healthy. Use boundaries for people who trigger you to minimize time in their presence or even set conversation guidelines.

Communicate your needs as clearly as possible, create time and space to take care of yourself, stick to your clear guidelines, and be willing to say no.

Determine Non-negotiables

We get up early, exercise twice a day, and go to bed early. We rarely allow anything to disrupt those parameters. It means that we have to let go of a lot of things. In order to live by that schedule, we don't have the opportunity to participate in a lot of evening social events. But to be perfectly honest, they no longer entice us much anyway.

Our schedule is part of our non-negotiables, along with eating a balanced diet and spending quality time with our kids. These non-negotiables set a baseline for all our decisions and lifestyle. It makes it easier to just follow those priorities and not get distracted by things that don't fit well with them. Any deviation from our non-negotiables usually results in regret afterward.

Get very clear on what your non-negotiables are for your day or your life, then be willing to let go of whatever doesn't cooperate.

Change Your Appearance

After we resolved to be new people with a new life, there was one thing holding me back—my reflection in the mirror. I wanted my new outlook to be reflected in my appearance. I wanted to look confident, fierce, and fun.

Luckily, my hairstylist Jen was up for the challenge. I told her to shave one side of my head and cut the rest into an asymmetrical diagonal. She handed me the hair clippers and let me take the first swipe. *Freedom!* What I didn't realize was that cutting my hair was like cutting the cords of the past. It was a ceremony to honor the new me and let go of the old.

Do something drastic with your appearance to embody the new feelings you want to radiate. Step into a new style and let go of the past.

Forgive

When I was a kid, I used to get really angry at my siblings for the usual stuff: taking my things, getting more than me, or putting in the last piece of the puzzle. But my younger brother and sister would either be oblivious or not care. My anger did not affect them; instead, it affected me and put me in a terrible mood. I would stew away in my room while they went on about their day.

Forgiveness is something that I have learned to do because I no longer want to carry those negative feelings. It does not mean that you accept the unjust actions of others, or that you allow other people to walk all over you. It means that you let go of the stress, dis-ease, and harm that it causes within you.

Forgive, so that you can move on and feel better. Let go of the negative thoughts and feelings it causes within.

Allow Yourself to Let Go and Live

When you feel stuck in your life, it's because you can't let go of the old and embrace the new. You are no longer growing. And when you stop growing, you start dying.

Take responsibility for the chains that are holding you down. The only person that can free yourself is you. Start working on yourself physically, mentally, emotionally, and spiritually. **Personal growth is the antidote for feeling stuck.** Then, if there are elements in your life that are holding you back, you have to be willing to let them go.

Letting go means standing up for yourself and following your own path. Trust that everything truly meant for you will evolve alongside you. And if it doesn't evolve with you, then you have to release it, remove it, or change it.

This goes for people as well. When you start changing your life, there are going to be people who protest. Never hold yourself back because it makes someone else feel better. Never hold yourself back because you feel guilty. Never hold yourself back to fit in. Trust that you will attract new people into your life who will accept and support the new you.

Letting go means that you are willing to grow and evolve. You can accept there is no going back to your old ways and your old identity. Enjoy the process of getting to know yourself better each day.

Letting go means you don't have to force, and you don't have to struggle. Your intuition will guide you and all of a sudden everything will feel right. The path that is truly meant for you will light up before your eyes. Life will be joyful.

Even though letting go feels scary in the moment, it will create freedom, inner peace, and massive personal growth. See your future self, and find the motivation to free that stunning person. Your full potential is waiting for you to release the chains holding you back.

The phone is ringing. Life as you know it is on the line, and your reaction will determine the future. You have two choices—you can hold on tight, keep yourself stuck, and deteriorate.

Or . . .

You can let go and grow into the person you were meant to be.

PHASE 5

Accelerate

CHAPTER 8

Accelerate

The Universe knows when you are ready.

I had butterflies in my stomach and my head felt light. Excitement and fear filled the air. This decision would take our habits and our lives to a drastic new level—a level that seemed way out of our league. Jake suggested we wait a few weeks to prepare so we could buy some new exercise gear, research our best options, plan our daily schedule, eat up the last of our junk food, and drink alcohol a few more times.

I stared back at him with a new fire kindling in my soul and said, "We need to start *now*."

Jake resisted for a moment, but he knew I was right.

So we set our alarm clock for 5 a.m. and jumped into a new routine—and a new life. We were starting a challenge called 75 Hard, based on a book by Andy Frisella.

For seventy-five days in a row, we would push ourselves to the limits thanks to Andy Frisela, who came up with this nightmare that slowly turns into euphoria. Here is a quick summary of the daily checklist so you know what we are referring to, but please research this program in more detail for yourself.

For seventy-five consecutive days, no exceptions, no pauses, no breaks:

* Complete two 45-minute workouts (one of them must be outdoors)
* Drink a gallon of water
* Follow a diet (of your own choosing)
* Eliminate alcohol
* No junk food or cheat meals
* Read ten pages of a personal development book
* Take a picture of yourself to document your progress

We had never dedicated that much time to ourselves before. It was thrilling to focus so much energy on our own health and personal development over work, chores, family, friends, and fun—over *everything*. We were about to prioritize ourselves in a whole new way. 75 Hard gave us a reason to stick to the extreme version of all the healthy habits we had always wanted but never had the courage or motivation to do on our own.

A lot of people thought we had gone off the deep end, and some days we wondered about our own sanity. Luckily the 75 Hard checklist helped justify our actions. If people questioned why we were going for a jog in the cold rain, we could say, "I have to get my outdoor workout done today." If people asked why we didn't eat a slice of birthday cake or drink a beer, we could say, "I can't because I'm doing 75 Hard right now." It was an easy answer for anyone who wondered why we would make those disturbing choices, especially when just a month or two ago we would have indulged. The program gave us an excuse when "working on ourselves" wasn't a good enough answer.

Forty-five days into the program, our diet started getting sloppy. There was too much gray area in the parameters we had chosen, and we started sliding back into bad habits. After eating at a questionable restaurant and feeling awful, we knew we had messed up past the breaking point. We couldn't mark the day as completed with a good conscience.

We failed. So . . .

We started over the very next morning back on day one, this time with a clearly defined diet to follow and keep us in line.

Our second attempt at 75 Hard sealed the deal on our new habits. We successfully completed the full seventy-five days in a row, and our new identity was imprinted into our cells. It wasn't just a physical change; it was a mental shift. We realized that prioritizing our health was the most important thing in our lives. And after completing 75 Hard, there was no going back.

Ever.

In fact, returning to our old life sounded much more painful than continuing with this new one.

Our family and friends were confused and disappointed. They had expected us to revert back to our old selves and previous lifestyle. But we couldn't. We had grown and evolved. When you follow healthy habits for that long, you see and feel the difference. You finally get to experience what it truly means to *feel good*. And you never want to return to how you felt before. Following the checklist every day was empowering, and seventy-five days in a row was life-changing. You follow through—even on the hard days, even when you don't feel like it, even when you don't think you deserve it, even when you are too busy.

Every day, every decision, every habit matters. Doing hard things in the moment makes your life easier.

Zoom Out to Focus On the Present

Our daily perspective is so small that it's difficult to widen the lens and see a lifetime of choices. We focus on satisfying our moment-to-moment desires and can't stop to recognize the impact those cravings have on our future.

Bad habits add up over time and result in health problems and misery. If we are making poor decisions that keep dragging us further from the person we want to become, then it is truly death by a thousand cuts. We are making the incisions ourselves, and we can't even acknowledge it.

All of your decisions and habits created the person you are right now.

All of your distractions kept you safe from facing the truth, but they also kept you from understanding what really matters—you.

You.

You matter more than anything. You matter more than your job, your bank account, your health insurance, your house, your status, your achievements, more than everything in your life.

But the true irony is that when you finally put yourself first, when you take care of yourself, spend time on yourself, respect yourself, and love yourself, then you will show up as your best self for everyone and everything else.

Stop being a martyr for the world.

It is not helping anyone—especially you. If you've had a rough day, a rough week, a rough year, or even a rough decade, you can still turn it around. You can change, no matter where you are or how old you are. If there is something you want to do or someone you want to be, now is your chance.

This chapter is going to push you. We are going to take everything to the extreme, just like 75 Hard. The action steps and advice in the previous chapters were just the beginning.

This is your warning.

Get ready to:

1. Prioritize Your Health Above All Else
2. Assemble a Mastermind
3. Conquer and Liberate Your Mindset
4. Believe Anything is Possible

If you are reading this, then the Universe believes you are ready. Challenge yourself and take your life to new heights.

1. Prioritize Your Health Above All Else

The better you feel, the better your entire life will become. Invest in your well-being and push your physical health to the max. Everything else will naturally follow. Once you experience and appreciate how good you can feel, you will never want to go back. Most people never realize what they are missing out on because they can't keep healthy habits long enough to experience the full benefits. Don't accept a mediocre life; step up to a better version of you with these action steps.

Raise Your Habits to the Next Level

Wes Watson of the GP Penitentiary *Life* podcast said, "Show me your habits, and I'll tell you your future." The level of your habits and daily choices will determine who you are and who you will become. I hope the 75 Hard Program sparked some curiosity within you. I bet you already know what I am going to tell you to do next.

Research the 75 Hard program developed by Andy Frisela, download the app, throw away your junk food and alcohol, brace yourself and your calendar, and start *now*.

Invest in Your Wellness

Like most people, we used to treat vacations like an overconsumption debauchery-fest. We would indulge in every way possible because that's what you do when you're on vacation. You overeat, drink all day, and lie around. But then when we got home, I always felt tired, gross, and my clothes didn't fit. The time away made coming back to reality that much harder.

I started wishing for a vacation that would allow me to feel better afterward. I wanted to feel refreshed, healthier, and energized when I got home. So on my list of future goals, I added "Attend a Wellness Retreat," even though I didn't really know what that meant.

When I first heard about yoga retreats, it was an exciting moment. This was what I was searching for! Not only did they offer yoga classes every day, but they were focused on health in a variety of ways. The price tag was no joke, and it was scary to invest that kind of money. So I used my fortieth birthday present to justify the expense. That trip ended up being one of the most important investments of my life.

Jake and I never regret investing in our well-being and our future. A year after my first yoga retreat, we realized how much that investment had paid off and decided to attend a yoga retreat together. That was when we met our shaman on the Greek Island. We spent a week on our physical and mental health, strengthening our relationship, and getting crystal clear on our future. It proved yet again the incredible value of spending vacation time as your best self instead of bloated, zoned out, and hung over.

Designate a vacation or book a retreat that improves your health, vitality, and personal development.

Challenge Your Fitness

Back in my twenties, I was so flippin' proud of myself when I signed up and completed my first 5K fun run. It was a challenge that got me excited to train, and the crowd really pumped me up. I was hooked. And it got me signed up for my first marathon in 2007. About twenty years later, the same thing happened to Jake. It was a huge challenge getting him signed up for his first 5K. But soon we were signing up for 10K's, then ten miles, and half marathons. Within about two years, he was signing up for his first full marathon. We also branched out and tried a Spartan Race and Tough Mudders.

The scariest part was signing up. Once you are committed, then the motivation kicks in to train and practice so you don't embarrass yourself. When you arrive at the start line, you realize that it isn't a competition at all. In fact, everyone is cheering each other on.

Sign up for a 5K, or a physically challenging event that you have never attempted before.

Try Extreme Meditation

Did you know that you could take meditation to the extreme? When Jake registered for a ten-day silent meditation course, I happily applauded him from the sideline. I have not had the courage to attend one myself, and many people in our life felt the same way. Others thought he was completely nuts.

Jake drove himself to a Vipassana Meditation Center, gave up his phone and car keys, and sat in stillness and silence for ten days. The meditation practice was only paused to sleep, eat, and occasionally clean. The busy world of distractions came to a screeching halt. Jake's thoughts, feelings, sensations, and observations intensified. He found joy in the strangest of things which he had never experienced before— like cleaning a bathroom. At one point he caught a glimpse of two ladybugs fighting, and it was as exciting as a *Gladiator* movie.

Jake had done some meditation on his own before, but this took it to an extreme level. He didn't know how loud the outside world had become inside his own head until it went quiet. Several people wanted to leave because it was so intense, but they were continually encouraged to stick it out. By day three, a couple of people couldn't take it anymore and left. By day four and five, the aura from each participant became almost tangible. Nonverbal communication between the participants became as loud and obvious as verbal communication.

Jake returned home in a blissful state with so many insights. His biggest takeaway was realizing how many distractions we have in our life. Even simple conversations can interrupt your focus, not to mention phones, screens, people, crowds, sights, sounds, smells, and all the external commotion we are subject to on a daily basis. It took about a week for Jake to slowly reintegrate into our busy world, and he needed a lot of extra sleep. But nothing seemed to bother him, and he even cleaned our bathroom!

Check out a Vipassana Meditation Course as taught by S.N. Goenka. We highly recommend practicing every day to build up your stamina, just like training for a marathon.

Harness Your Life Force

What is your life force exactly? It's your breath. For almost forty years of my life, I had no idea how powerful breathing was. It was something I took for granted and never thought much about. I assumed it was one of those autopilot bodily functions that took care of itself. But that all changed when I heard Wim Hof on one of my regular podcasts. He was passionately explaining a breathing technique that could snap you into a meditative state, relieve stress, and help heal the body. I was super intrigued and wanted to try it for myself.

Jake did his usual online research and found a YouTube video tutorial by Wim Hof that we could follow along. It was a strange exercise, and we would have been embarrassed if anyone had walked in unannounced. I lay flat on the floor and breathed as deeply as possible for thirty reps, then held my breath for thirty to ninety seconds. In this video, he talked us through three rounds. My body and brain started tingling. I could feel my heartbeat and my blood circulating. I lost track of time. It was magical.

We enjoyed the video so much that we downloaded the app. Then we could customize our experience in a variety of ways and hold our breath as long as we wanted. I use this breathing technique especially when I have a headache, feel stressed out, or overwhelmed. It instantly calms me down and puts me into a better mindset. If there are parts of me that are injured or not feeling well, those particular areas get warm and feel better afterward. I always end the session wondering why I don't do it more often. There are times that we have included this breathing exercise into our morning routine, and it has been very powerful.

Try Wim Hof's guided breathing exercise on YouTube. (Search for *Wim Hof Method Guided Breathing for Beginners*.) Or download the *Wim Hof Method Breathing & Cold* app for a customized experience. You may have to get over feeling silly, embarrassed, or scared, but anyone can try it as long as you have a safe and comfortable environment.

Refine Your Diet

A few days before opening night and my debut as Maria in *The Sound of Music*, Jake started getting low heart rate alarms from his smartwatch. He had been feeling very fatigued and light-headed, so he went to a walk-in clinic to get it checked out. They assessed his condition and sent him to the emergency room. He was hooked up to a heart rate monitor while the doctors tried to figure out the cause. But they couldn't find anything. He didn't fit the normal patient stereotype now that he was in the average weight category, exercised everyday, and ate a super clean diet. So eventually they just sent him home without answers.

I was frustrated that he would choose this week—the most important week of the year for me—to have a major health emergency. I had been rehearsing for months and working so hard for the upcoming musical, and he was supposed to be supporting me, not the other way around. I didn't have an understudy and the show would not go on without me. So I had to leave Jake to fend for himself while I tried to block out my concern and guilt.

Even though the doctors couldn't provide a diagnosis, something was severely wrong, so Jake started researching online. When he figured out the answer, it made so much sense. It was a lack of protein in his diet. Jake had been cutting back on calories to lose weight and was eating mostly fruits and vegetables at the expense of protein. His body was literally eating itself from the inside to make up for the deficiency. Jake found an app to log his food and track his macronutrients: protein, fat, and carbohydrates. He adjusted his diet to be more balanced, and within a few days he felt better. The fatigue and dizziness vanished. He started building back his muscle, and his heart rate returned to normal.

We had taken our diet to the opposite extreme without all the knowledge we needed. We were so obsessed with calorie-in, calorie-out, that we weren't listening to all the obvious cues that Jake's body was trying to send him.

Balance your diet, and listen to your body. Find an app to log your food for a few days that includes macronutrients. Don't get obsessed like we did; just use the information to get a general sense of where you are so you can make adjustments if needed. We started with CarbManager, but I am sure there are a lot of options out there. Once you find a good balance of different types of food that fuel your body in a healthy way, stop tracking and let your body do the talking. Then make sure you listen.

2. Assemble a Mastermind

There are people out there who can help you reach your full potential. You don't have to do everything by yourself. When you find and surround yourself with the right people, it makes life easier, more fun, and more fulfilling. Here are a few ideas to get your community started.

Absorb Awesomeness

One of the people I looked up to most during high school was my violin teacher, Paula. She was mindful and intelligent, not to mention a skilled teacher and talented musician. She taught violin using the Suzuki Method, which means she started kids very young and it immersed them into music, similar to learning language. When our first daughter Avery was three years old, we jumped at the chance to sign her up for lessons with Paula. We were very excited about the influence she would have on our daughter. Learning to play the violin was a beautiful part of Avery's development, but what mattered even more was the dedicated time and mentoring she received each week.

There have been many people in our lives with this same kind of power and magnetism. It makes us want to learn anything and everything from them. We jump at whatever chance presents itself and don't question the specifics. You know that simply being with them is the right thing to do.

Take a class or join an activity simply because you respect the teacher or the other participants. Absorb their good energy and allow it to influence your life. Be open to receive the knowledge, experience, and opportunity that comes your way.

Choose Your Circle

During college, we were surrounded by inspiring professors and ambitious friends, and it propelled us upward. It was a major growing point in our lives and we wanted that momentum back. We didn't realize it until recently, but the people we spent the most time with were the biggest indicators of where our lives were headed. Now we use that knowledge to choose our relationships wisely and be intentional about who is influencing our future.

You are the sum of the five people you spend the most time with. No matter what you think about those people or how you feel about them, their presence impacts you. You will slowly become like them whether you like it or not. It is important to be very deliberate about your relationships, and who you are allowing to impact your life.

Who are the five people that you spend the most time with? Be intentional about who they are and it will decide who you become.

Hire a Coach

Jake and I always struggle to reach out for help. We try to figure everything out on our own and toil away from start to finish. We think we have to do everything ourselves, but it gets overwhelming. When we finally reach our breaking point and invest in a coach or expert, the investment always pays off.

The most successful people in any field assemble a team to help them in a variety of areas. They can acknowledge that they don't know everything and need guidance and coaching from experts. If we can put our ego aside and learn from others who already have the knowledge or skills, life becomes so much easier. We don't have to know everything and do everything ourselves. We will be more successful and get there so much more quickly if we rely on others to help us. And the time and money you invest in those experts will come right back to you.

Hire a coach and stop trying to do everything on your own.

Life Coach

While we were still at the farm and at the peak of our internal struggle, we stepped outside of our comfort zone and hired a life coach, Julie. Before that, I had no idea what a life coach was and thought it was ridiculous. I thought living your life was something that just happened to you. But after meeting an inspiring person who offered that specialty, we wanted to try it out. Julie helped us set goals, focus our lives, work on our weaknesses, lean into our strengths, evaluate the path, and kept us accountable. We were so fortunate to have Julie coach us through some very crucial months.

I have made a complete 180 about the necessity of a life coach. Nothing is more important than getting your life on track. When other specialists focus on a single area, a life coach can take a holistic approach. They can help you gain insight into how all the pieces fit together and then you can take intentional action in the direction you want to go.

If you are ready to make meaningful changes in your life, hire a life coach. The right one is out there waiting for you.

Fitness Coach

When I joined my local functional fitness gym, I just wanted to balance out my running with some cross training. I had no idea that I was also hiring an amazing fitness coach. Jeff not only led the group workouts, but he offered individual advice and personalized options for each move. He made sure that every athlete was performing the moves with proper technique and alignment for optimal results and to minimize the risk of injury. He had a wealth of knowledge that could be applied at the gym and used to recuperate at home. Even when I was injured or recovering from surgery, I would go to the gym, and he would offer advice for modifying exercises or DIY physical therapy.

I learned so much about fitness, strength training, nutrition, and recovery. It improved my health and entire exercise routine. When we moved, I was really sad to leave the gym, my fitness coach Jeff, and all my fellow athletes behind, but I was so grateful for all the knowledge I could bring with me.

Hire a fitness coach, start going to an exercise class, or join a sports team where a coach can help you.

Career Coach

Writing a book was something we always wanted to do, but it was too overwhelming to ever get started. Even though we felt compelled to tell our story, we couldn't do it on our own. There was way too much to figure out. Then just as fate would have it, we were at a conference and found StoryBuilders. It flung the doors wide open. We didn't have to know everything about the business to write a book and get it published—they could help us through the process.

We hired StoryBuilders to bring our story out into the world. We have been meeting with a team of people every few weeks to coach us through the writing process and work on all the logistics to keep the project going. This book, the one you are reading right now, would have never happened without hiring them and relying on their skills, knowledge, and network.

If you have a specific career goal, hire someone who can teach you or walk you through the process. You don't have to do everything on your own. You will reach your goals much more easily and successfully with a coach.

Any Kind of Coach

There's no limit to coaches. I could keep telling you about how different types of coaches have helped us, but I think you get the point. No matter what area you are struggling in, there is an expert out there who can help you. Some of the other most common types are: financial advisors, business/marketing consultants, relationship coaches, dieticians/nutritional coaches, and health and wellness coaches.

Hire someone to help you. Whether you are looking for a general coach or a very specific one, you can find the perfect fit.

Join Motivational Groups

When we moved off the farm and into a nearby town, Jake joined a local running group. Jake and I had always run by ourselves, so this was a fun new concept for us.

Every Saturday morning, the group would plan a meeting place and run a few miles together. It was really motivating for Jake to have a group of people (not just me!) who encouraged his healthy habits. And I'm sure you can imagine the type of people who participated. They were optimistic, fun-loving, active people. Not only was it motivating for Jake to keep up his exercise habits, but they all became friends, talked about their lives, and inspired each other in a large variety of ways.

Even after moving away, he still checks in on the group once in a while, and it keeps him motivated even from thousands of miles away.

Join a group that keeps you motivated to continue your healthy habits.

3. Conquer and Liberate Your Mindset

When we stopped playing the victim of our situation, we realized that there was nothing physically holding us back. Everything came from our minds. The chains were our thoughts and beliefs. We finally freed ourselves by opening our minds, challenging our limiting beliefs, changing our perspective, and focusing on the positives. Our minds started growing. We started taking control of our thoughts, and responsibility for our lives. Then we found these empowering ways to take it up another notch.

Be Grateful and Learn from Every Experience

When Jake and I have a hard day or a difficult experience, the mantra that helps us the most is, **"This is the experience I need right now."** We repeat it over and over in our heads and even out loud. It reminds us that we can learn and grow from any situation we are in, and the harder it is, the more we can learn and grow from it. It reminds us to detach and reflect as an observer. It reminds us that it's temporary, and we will come out on the other side as ourselves again. It reminds us that life's challenges will teach us to be better people. It reminds us to find gratitude for the change it will spark in our lives.

Jake and I would not replace or alter our story for anything. We needed the pain and suffering to create the people we are today. We would've never uncovered the path to our true purpose or highest potential. We would've never had the courage to risk everything and follow our dreams. Instead of being angry at the world for the challenges we have faced, we are beyond grateful for the lessons we learned, the shock it caused to our systems, and the outcome of who and where we are today.

If you are having a bad day or a difficult experience, remind yourself, "This is the experience I need right now." Find the life lesson it is teaching you and look forward to the person you will become on the other side.

Become the Leading Actor in Your Life Drama

I thought I was the least important person within Rieke Farms because I was an in-law, a woman, a part-time employee, and the youngest of all the owners. I allowed it to be my reality for many years. I didn't speak up in meetings because I didn't think I was important enough, so I provided the refreshments instead of my ideas.

The moment I started seeing myself differently was the moment people started treating me differently. My time, my future, and my life were just as important as everyone else's. The first meeting that I attended with this new mindset was glorious. I held my head up high, looked people directly in the eyes, voiced my opinion whenever I felt compelled, and commanded the respect of the room.

The external world is a mirror of what is going on in our minds. People will only treat you as well as you believe you should be treated. When you take time to raise your self-worth, it will be reflected in everything around you. You can choose to be the leading actor of your life, or you can choose to be a stagehand.

Value yourself, confidently step into the spotlight, and then soak in the applause. This is your life and you can choose to be the star.

Open Your Mind to Creativity

Creativity is not limited to art. In fact, I believe that Jake is much more creative than I am, even though I'm labeled an "artist." It's his new and exciting ideas that make him uber-creative. He is able to open his mind and allow thoughts to flow to him without judging them or brushing them off for logistical reasons. He is open to all possibilities instead of narrowing his mind to a single solution. I am constantly amazed at the number of ideas he is able to tune in to.

I am slowly learning ways to open my mind to new ideas and solutions. There are certain times of day and certain activities that spark my creativity. Mornings in particular are a much more creative time of day for me. I am also more open to ideas after exercising or breathwork. So I do my best to prioritize projects that require the most creativity (like writing this book!) during the morning hours or just after a motivating activity.

Creative ideas can also pop up when you least expect them, and it's important to quickly jot them down so you don't forget them. Sometimes it's in the middle of the night, or sometimes it's during a shower. One book that really inspired me on the subject of creative thinking was *Big Magic* by Elizabeth Gilbert, which I highly recommend.

Everyone is creative; it's a matter of tuning in to the ideas and having an open mind. Explore the times of day and activities that bring out the most creativity for you.

4. Believe Anything is Possible

Now that you have conquered and liberated your mindset, there is nothing out of reach. You can take steps toward any goal, any dream, any life, and any person that you want to become. Allow your new mindset to motivate you into action toward a beautiful, limitless future.

Set Monumental Goals

When we started setting goals, we started moving the needle. Before that, we were simply living day by day, expecting life to improve, and wondering why nothing ever changed. It was because we didn't have any specific goals to work toward. So we sat down together and wrote goals for every area of our life. Only then could we actually work toward them and make progress. We set fitness, career, financial, relationship, and family goals. We also set travel and recreational goals. Then we brainstormed ways to work toward them. It worked. Our lives finally moved forward.

Setting goals is a really important step toward changing your life. If you don't know the outcome you are looking for, then there is no way to ever get there. One of the most important things our life coach did with us was get very specific with our goals. We came up with yearly, monthly, weekly, and daily timelines that kept us on schedule for reaching each of our goals. We got laser-focused and specific.

Set goals for the next one, five, and ten years that include all areas of your life (health, fitness, family, career, social, financial, recreational, etc). Break them down into a timeline, or start taking action steps toward them even if you don't know the full path forward yet.

Visualize Your Dream Life

After attending my first yoga retreat in Costa Rica, I had one prominent thought running through my head. *I want to live at a yoga retreat in Costa Rica.* It wouldn't go away, and I believed it was possible.

I didn't know exactly how we would get there or when it would happen; I just knew that it was my dream life. I knew that it would happen someday. I expected that it would take a while, maybe a decade. But it came sooner than I ever imagined possible.

The day came only a year and a half after that pure belief entered my system. I am proof that visualizing your dream life works. We now live in a condominium in Costa Rica that feels *exactly* like a yoga resort.

Vision boards have also been a very powerful tool for us. We like to find or print pictures that have inspiring images of our goals and dreams, then we tape them to our mirror. Every time we look at ourselves, we see those images at the same time. When we reach or modify our goals, we take them down and replace them with new images. It keeps us motivated and excited for what's to come.

Visualize your dream life and believe it will happen someday. Use your imagination to focus on it as often as possible, or create a vision board by hanging pictures of your dream life where you will see them every day.

Raise Your Vibration

Everything is made up of energy. Humans are no different. Even though we feel like solid, separate beings, at the most basic level, we are energy. All the choices we make either raise or lower our vibration. When we make healthy choices, think positive thoughts, and treat people with respect and love, it raises our vibrational frequency, and we feel better.

Those good vibes attract more good things into your life. Like attracts like. When you are joyful, grateful, peaceful, and loving, then you receive more of those into your life. Everything you send out returns to you.

Raise your vibration with healthy habits, positive thoughts, and being kind to others. When you feel good, you will attract more good things into your life.

Strive for Self-Realization

Remember when we talked about *Maslow's Hierarchy of Needs* in Chapter 4?

We hope that the action steps and ideas we have offered since then have helped you build a solid foundation and move up in the triangle. Every day and every moment will feel different, and there is never a finish line. There are times when you will have to return to each of the levels to support your journey. Keep working, and keep building.

After you have your foundational needs met, we want you to strive for the top: Self-Actualization. You deserve to achieve your full potential, and the world needs you to serve your life's purpose.

Live Right Now

You are going to die. This is it. This is the life you get.

Live your life now, while you still can. Try everything. Don't hold yourself within an imaginary box that you will regret or resent. Even if something seems too extreme or too crazy, just go for it. It doesn't matter how old you are or where you are in your life right now. This is the perfect time for you to follow your dreams and become the person you were meant to be. No excuses.

Never stop growing and building. There is no finish line to the action steps we have listed here for you. If you complete 75 Hard, move on to the next phase! Yes, there are more phases after that. If you complete a marathon, try a triathlon! When something on your vision board becomes a reality in your life, replace the picture with something even greater! Keep pushing yourself to new levels in every area. Never settle. This is the time to accelerate your life.

Prioritize your health above all else. Raise all your habits to the next level with 75 Hard. Invest in your wellness with vacations that make you feel better. Challenge your fitness with fun runs, marathons, Spartan Races, or Tough Mudders. Try extreme meditation with a Silent Meditation course. Harness your life force with Wim Hof's breathing exercises. Refine your diet by tracking your macronutrients and listening to your body.

Assemble a mastermind. Absorb awesomeness from amazing people, and intentionally choose who you surround yourself with. Hire a coach to teach you, guide you, and keep you accountable (life, fitness, career, and more). Join motivational groups to keep you going in the direction you want to go.

Conquer and liberate your mindset. Be grateful and learn from every experience by using the mantra, "This is the experience I need right now." Be the leading actor of your life drama and value yourself like the showstopping star that you are. Be creative and allow ideas to flow into your life.

Believe anything is possible. Set goals, break them down into smaller steps, and start moving. Visualize your dream life by focusing on it every day, creating vision boards, and knowing that it is on the way. Raise your vibration with a healthy body and a healthy mind, and treat others with love and respect. Strive for self-actualization to fulfill your purpose and reach your full potential.

This is your life. It is your most precious possession. Start treating it that way. Invest everything you can in yourself right now.

When you become the best version of yourself, you will serve the world in marvelous ways. Your kids, your family, your friends, and your community need you right now.

There is a fire in your soul that knows you were meant for great things. You know deep down all the things you should be doing, so start following your intuition. Every day, every moment, every tiny decision matters.

The Universe knows that you are ready. It's time to step up.

PHASE 6

Navigate

CHAPTER 9

Navigate

I stared at the bass guitar player from across the high school band room. He was confident, fun, a free thinker, and a rebel. He commanded respect as the student council president but boldly questioned authority at the same time. He was a football player, a musician, and a smokin' hot high school senior.

I was a "goody-goody" junior playing the marimba in the back of the room. Learning came easily for me, but the social part did not. I felt awkward and intimidated around the majority of my classmates. I had low self-esteem and hid my face full of acne as best as I could.

He was *way* out of my league.

But I couldn't help it.

I felt drawn to him. I wanted to be like him and be with him, so I stared at him from across the band room every day. I started modifying my routes to class so we could cross paths in the hallway. I freshened my makeup, tried to act as cool as I could, and made eye contact with him whenever possible.

Our lives seemed to intertwine more and more—jazz band, pop choir, orchestra. I was even voted into the student council in a special seat as the band representative.

The more time I spent near him, the more I worked to live up to his standards. I had no choice but to rise to his level because I wanted more than anything to be with him.

Slowly, he started noticing me, and it motivated me even more. My efforts were paying off! Then, miraculously, he started feeling the connection too. He began going out of his way to spend more time with me in return. The momentum inevitably brought us together.

We started dating, and I was walking on air. It catapulted my personal development even further. By the following year, I had become a confident, fun, free-thinking, rebel senior—just like him. Not only that, but my boyfriend was now a college freshman, which boosted my status and self-worth even further. I felt like a smokin' hot senior.

Jake's influence changed me.

Well, not exactly.

To word it more accurately, Jake's influence motivated me to grow and elevate. I had done the work, and as a result, the team we created was powerful. We had so much potential!

Over the next few years, we grew together. We went to neighboring universities and welcomed knowledge, friends, and new experiences. We pushed each other to try new things and conquer challenges. The world was wide open, and anything was possible. We got married after college, coasted through our twenties, and ended the decade with a two-year adventure in the Peace Corps El Salvador.

Losing Ground

When we returned from our service abroad, we allowed society's expectations of "settling down" to permeate our lives. We lost our sense of adventure, freedom, creativity, and fun. We focused on the wrong things and let our health and personal lives get off course. Trouble started between us when Jake hit a serious downturn. Secretly, I blamed myself, since I was his life partner and had been by his side. I worried that it was my presence and influence that had caused his slump into depression. So I followed him down.

I was desperate to fix it. I thought since we were a team, I should share his regression. It was only fair for me to work as hard as he did, suffer as much as he did, and skip holidays and vacations like he did. But that only made things worse—much, much worse.

It was the opposite of high school where Jake had motivated me to grow. At this point in our relationship, Jake's influence was motivating me to slide backward. Life was closing in, and we felt isolated from knowledge, friends, experiences, and adventures. Our relationship was no longer fun and exciting. It was draining and painful.

Our personal development came to a crashing halt and then hit a downward spiral. When we stopped growing, our marriage started tearing apart. We barely held it together for many years, and it took both of us to repair all the damage.

We had to figure out how to navigate our relationship up and out of a precarious mess. We each had different challenges to overcome, along with different perspectives, expectations, needs, wants, limiting beliefs, goals, strengths, and weaknesses. We needed each other's care and support in very different ways. Many of the lessons came as a huge surprise at first, but now they make so much sense.

In high school, developing ourselves and our relationship came so easily. We wanted each other, and we wanted the world. But over the years we got too comfortable, too lazy, and we took each other for granted.

So if we still wanted, more than anything, to be with each other—then we would have to work for it. So that's exactly what we did. And learning how to navigate our relationship was the ultimate key that unlocked our lives.

When we are united, we are unstoppable.

Lessons Learned

Welcome to the final phase of The Brilliant Life Journey. If you're here, you made it through the first five phases: Contemplate, Investigate, Activate, Eliminate, and Accelerate. Those chapters were all about you. We hope that you know yourself better and that you continue to discover the best version of yourself. Now it's time to open back up to the world as your awesome unique self and navigate your relationships.

There are four distinct areas in the Navigation Phase:

1. Own Your Side
2. Support Their Side
3. Power Up
4. Unite with Integrity

If you are in a marriage or long-term relationship, then this phase is especially important. The relationship you have with your partner affects every aspect of your life. If you start growing without them, then you will start growing apart. We hope that these insights will strengthen your connection, attraction, power, and potential as a team. You can also apply the following action steps to support any relationship—our advice is not limited to married couples. In fact, some of our examples come from experiences with our kids.

Your life partner, your family, and your friends should propel your life upward. They should be your source of joy, love, hope, and peace. They are the key to unlocking the world in new and exciting ways you could have never even imagined on your own.

1. Own Your Side

I thought Jake was in a slump and needed to change. I thought Jake was depressed, but that *I* was just fine. I thought Jake was making unhealthy lifestyle choices, but that *I* was doing everything right. I believed that I was the strong one holding it all together. What I failed to see was that I needed as much help as he did. I was an equal contributor to our dysfunctional lives.

The first thing we both had to do was turn inward instead of pointing fingers. We each played a part in the relationship we were trying to fix and had to take responsibility for it. We had to change how we were showing up for each other.

Take Control of You

I used to be a control freak. I told everyone what to do, when to do it, exactly how to do it, and corrected them if it wasn't just right. Jake once said he felt like he was living under a constant hum of pressure. It raised the anxiety level of everyone in our household, including my own.

My need to control my husband's and my children's lives was the result of feeling out of control of my own. I felt like I was at the mercy of our busy schedule and mountain of responsibilities. I didn't think I had time to do anything for myself. Trying to control others was my solution to gaining control of my own life.

Then I heard the mantra, "I control my time." It was really hard to believe at first. Since starting a family, I thought I had given up control of my time. I thought I was being whisked around all day by my family responsibilities, chores, and work. I was being a martyr, just like Jake, and I didn't even realize it.

I started using that mantra whenever I felt out of control. When I felt like a chauffeur, a servant, or a housekeeper, I would pause and calmly say, "I control my time." Then if what I was doing was important to me, I would continue with a much better attitude. If it wasn't important to me, I would decide to spend my time differently. It helped me realize that I wasn't living under a ruthless master called time and was actually in control. Even if someone convinced me or guilted me into doing something, it was ultimately still my decision to follow through.

Stop trying to control others; it will only push them away and increase everyone's stress. Instead, find the area of your life where you feel out of control, and start using a mantra to declare the opposite. It could be your time, energy, career, life choices, etc. Start telling yourself that you control it because you actually do.

Take Care of You

Jake is an extreme people-pleaser. He puts everything above his own needs and completely loses touch with himself. In the past, he thought he was doing the right thing by sacrificing himself for his family's legacy and providing a good quality of life for his wife and kids. But he was miserable and resentful, and all of his relationships suffered. During the rare times that he saw his kids, he was exhausted and grumpy.

When he started taking care of himself, he showed up as a better version of himself, and his relationships improved. He took time to exercise, eat healthier, be with his kids, read, find fun hobbies, socialize, and relax. Prioritizing his health and his needs wasn't selfish at all. It helped everyone and everything around him. He was happier at home and more productive at work.

Take care of yourself first, and do the things that are right for you. Only then will you be able to take care of others in the best possible way.

Always Move Upward

When Jake was stressed out, depressed, and toiling away on the farm, I held myself to the same standards. I didn't allow myself to be happier or take time to do things that made me feel good because I didn't think it was fair to him. But I was actually holding both of us back. Jake needed me to rise up and set a good example for him.

When I started making healthy decisions for myself, it positively affected both of us. My transformation inspired Jake to make changes for himself. My strength and stability held the family together. My positivity helped him through the slumps he encountered. I had been holding myself back because I thought it was better for him when I should have been doing the opposite.

After learning this about myself, I saw the pattern in all my relationships. If my family and friends were struggling, I thought I should struggle too. I had been intentionally holding myself back my entire life because I didn't want others to feel bad, and I wanted to fit in. But, the sense of community I received was shallow because the person who fit in wasn't the real me. On top of that, it was painful when I wasn't living up to my full potential. I finally acknowledged that holding myself back wasn't worth it. I also found out very quickly who was happy for me and who was resentful, and it ended up being a natural way to weed out toxic people and relationships. I could finally live authentically and unapologetically, and the new connections I made with people were genuine.

Don't hold yourself back or try to fit in. Live up to your full potential and inspire the people around you to rise up. Let go of those who do not support the best version of you.

Increase Your Magnetism

Jake and I used all the action steps from this book to become better people and raise our individual vibrations. We were healthier, physically fit, and energized. We were confident, more emotionally grounded, and we treated others better. The aura surrounding us became elevated and positive. We started attracting good things and good people into our lives.

Our attraction to each other rekindled. We were like magnets, feeling the pull back together. But it was much more than a physical attraction; it was a deeper chemistry of our souls. Our physical appearance and attraction were simply a reflection of the work we were doing from the inside out.

Use the action steps from the previous chapters to raise your vibration, strengthen the attraction you feel with your life partner, and magnetize positive people and experiences into your life. If there are some that you skipped, this could be the reason to push yourself a bit more.

2. Support Their Side

After you have taken responsibility for your side of the relationship, you can support others in a healthy way. Give them the space and tools to grow in their own unique manner and at their own pace. How you treat them along the way will make all the difference.

Empower Their Independence

Our first daughter, Avery, had extreme stranger anxiety for the first four years of her life. She was scared of everyone, everything, and clung to me constantly. It made our lives so difficult that we finally brought her to a therapist. Within a few minutes of the very first appointment, he could see the situation clearly. There was nothing wrong with her. The problem was simply how I was treating her.

I was doing EVERYTHING for her. I was acting like her personal attendant: waiting on her hand and foot, hauling around everything she might possibly want in a giant bag, carrying her if she got tired, consoling her if she was upset, answering every question, solving every problem, and responding immediately to all of her wants and needs. We still had a baby monitor in her bedroom so that if she needed anything during the night, she could tell us through the intercom and we would come running. She had never learned to do anything on her own.

The therapist encouraged us to start with easy things at home to empower her independence. We taught her how to take care of herself, like brushing her hair and teeth. We expected her to clean up her toys and help with family chores. We made her carry her own backpack if we left the house. We took the baby monitor out of her bedroom, and she had to get her own cup of water if she was thirsty. She protested the changes at first, but the long-term effects were empowering. Her independence generated confidence around new people and situations, and I was finally able to leave her at preschool without crying or clinging.

In the same sense, I was treating Jake the same way. I was doing everything for him and trying to take care of him way too much. I did it all out of pure love, but it wasn't healthy for me to be his everything—his best buddy, therapist, caretaker, cook, cleaner, advisor, and entertainer. I was exhausting myself and creating an unhealthy dependency.

Jake had to learn how to take care of himself. I had to start teaching him how to cook, clean, take care of our daughters, make friends, and live a healthy grown-up life. Taking more responsibility for his life raised his self-worth and gave his life more direction and meaning. He felt empowered to take on even more.

Encourage independence and problem-solving. If you do it all for them then they will never learn. Allow people to take care of themselves, think for themselves, solve problems, and learn.

Find The Good

Our second daughter, Maya, began cello lessons when she was four years old. Needless to say, it required a lot of parental involvement for the first couple of years. Practice time was always a challenge and seemed to get more and more difficult. I would try to help by telling her what to correct. This only annoyed her, and she would purposely play worse. She would play as fast and as sloppy as possible then look at me defiantly, both of us knowing that it was a hot mess. If I dared to say anything, it would shut her down completely. I didn't know what to do.

After attending a presentation by Ed Sprunger, author of *Helping Parents Practice*, I asked for his professional opinion. He sympathized with me and validated my position and dedication. Then he told me, no matter what happens, just find something to compliment. Anything. Don't try to correct or make improvements. Only focus on something good no matter how small.

The first few practice sessions this way were tough. I had to get really creative to find anything to compliment. But the more I focused on complimenting her, the more I found. And Maya started to play better without any of my critiques. She didn't need me to improve her, she just needed some encouragement.

When I had only criticized, she purposely gave me more to criticize. When I started complimenting, she gave me more to compliment. It all hinged on how I treated her and what I pointed out. This works with every relationship. If you are annoyed at all the things your spouse does wrong, start complimenting them on what they do well. If you are frustrated with your kids for everything they forget to do, start complimenting them when they remember. If you are frustrated with the way people act, start complimenting them on their unique strengths.

Focus on the good qualities and behaviors of others, then point them out with gratitude and amazement. Watch how it blossoms into more and more good things to compliment.

Show, Don't Tell

In the past, I didn't think that I should do anything fun if Jake didn't come with me. So I would either drag him along and he would resent it, or I wouldn't go and then regret it. It was a lose-lose situation.

When I finally started doing the things I wanted to do and leaving him behind, it was actually much better for both of us. I started joining in social events, family celebrations, and vacations, and let him stay home and work. I stopped forcing him to come, and the guilt of his absence faded with a little practice. Eventually, he felt left out and started joining me more often.

I have learned to give Jake the time and space to make his own decisions. Sometimes I leave an open-ended invitation without judgment or guilt as best as I can. Sometimes I don't even ask and just let him find the way on his own. I much prefer that he make the right decisions for himself, and we both feel better about it.

When I was preparing for my yoga retreat to Costa Rica, Jake could feel how excited I was to go, and then he witnessed how much I benefited from the experience. When I signed up for a yoga retreat in Greece the following year, he decided to join me.

Follow the path that is right for you and be a role model for others. Invite them to join you without judgment, respect their decision, and then share your results. Be patient—very, very patient. This process could take months (even years) for someone to follow your example.

Hold Space

Sometimes Jake gets trapped in a bad mood. Sometimes I get frustrated at people for being trapped in a bad mood and not doing anything about it. Then I absorb the bad mood. It's not an easy combination.

I was once at an MBSR (Mind Body Spirit Release) appointment and feeling annoyed with Jake's lingering bad mood. His negativity would permeate the household and spread to the rest of us. The practitioner listened and helped me into a healthier mindset by saying that she felt empathy for the negativity that Jake was dealing with. All of a sudden I saw Jake in a new light. His bad mood was not part of his identity. He was processing the negative energy just like I was, and I started appreciating everything he was going through.

Jake and I have had to learn and accept that we handle emotions differently. Jake uses his state of mind, meditation, and philosophy to work through them. I need to tune into my body and rely on physical practices like yoga and exercise, and I also have to set boundaries with negative people. We each have to find our own healthy ways of processing emotions, and we have to understand that we are each working through them even if it looks different from the outside.

Show empathy, have patience, listen, accept people for who they are, and allow them to work through life experiences in their own way. Do not feel obligated to absorb their negativity. If their bad mood starts bringing you down, then step away and find an activity that will raise you back up again.

3. Power Up

Now the magic really starts. After you have found ways to support yourself and your partner successfully, you can dig deep into the inner workings of the relationship. If you truly work together, both of your lives will elevate in ways that would never be possible on your own.

Serve Unconditionally

I used to be obsessed with "fair," and it caused me to see all my relationships as transactional. I expected that everything I contributed would be reciprocated equally. This was especially important to me in our marriage. If one of us was working, then the other should be working. If one of us spent a certain amount of money, the other should spend the same amount. If I planned a special birthday for him, then he should obviously do the same for me. When Jake, or anyone, did not live up to my imaginary guidelines of "fair," I was crushed. My expectations took all the love and kindness out of my relationships.

I had to learn how to let go of the transactional mindset to level up all my relationships. First, I started doing things for myself that I needed. Once my own cup was full, then I did not rely on others to fill those voids. It no longer felt like I was sacrificing myself to help someone else. I was gladly helping or supporting them, and I did not expect anything in return. Contributing to my relationships became joyful.

If you find yourself keeping score in your relationships, start by doing things for yourself that you expect others to do for you. After your needs are met, you can serve others without any expectations.

Align Your Goals

Our lives skyrocketed when Jake and I first sat down and wrote out our goals together. We discussed our individual goals, the goals we had as a team, and how they could support each other. The more aligned and focused we got, the more inspired we were to work toward them. We looked back at that list a year later, and those lofty dreams and goals had all come true! It was so shockingly powerful, that we now set goals together all the time.

Almost every morning we discuss what our goals are for the coming day. Every few weeks we sit down and review our monthly goals for the next four months. Every year we discuss and write down our goals for the coming year and the next ten years. Our focused energy of two people multiplies our power to achieve them.

Take time to discuss and write out your shared goals for the future with your life partner. You could also try the personal values cards from Chapter 4 and design your goals with both of your top values in mind. Make sure you are both equally involved and supported.

Divide and Conquer

Jake used to feel competitive in our marriage. His ego was a bit fragile, and he didn't like if there were things that I could do better than him. But he was forgetting about all the value he was bringing to our relationship that I could not.

We have learned to lean into our unique strengths. Jake is the ideas person, and I am the creation person. Jake comes up with so many new, fresh ideas that I actually have to slow him down sometimes. Then I take those gold mines and put them into action. This is why I'm the one who is physically writing this book even though he has an equally important part in it.

We don't have to do all the same things or be good at all the same things. It's actually better when we excel in different areas and widen our areas of expertise. Then, when we have a shared goal, we can divide the tasks to fit our strengths, and we accomplish so much more.

Focus on your unique strengths, and remind your partner of theirs. Then put them together and work toward a shared life vision.

Grow Exponentially Together

Jake and I have had seasons of personal development and seasons of feeling stuck. Experiencing them as a couple amplifies the excitement or the tension. When we were both feeling stuck in life, our marriage crumbled. Without any growth or support from each other, our relationship seemed to drain the last bit of life out of us.

Working on ourselves individually and then taking time every day to strengthen our bond created a wave of momentum that was stronger than we could have ever imagined. We got up early and spent our mornings together with exercise, meaningful discussions, and breakfast. In the evenings, we went for walks, hikes, practiced yoga, or read side by side. We took on challenges like 75 Hard, fun runs, and new eating habits. We made it on the other side of some extreme situations and stress, and now we can laugh about it, learn from mistakes, and grow.

We continue to encourage each other and push each other like teammates. It amplifies our high vibes and positive attraction. It glides us through all the ups and downs of life. We can rely on each other during difficult days, and boost each other further when we are on a roll. We understand the challenges and believe in each other more than anything.

Spend quality time with your life partner or the people you are closest to. Find healthy activities that you can share everyday: go for walks, exercise, read, get into nature, enjoy a sunset or sit down for a family meal. Take on challenges as a team and push each other to grow physically, mentally, emotionally, and spiritually. Encourage each other's personal development and discuss it regularly. Once you are aligned in an upward direction, anything is possible.

4. Unite with Integrity

It is easy for our emotions or egos to take control. No matter what stage our relationship is in, even a single conversation can trigger us or get out of hand. Take a step back, listen to your intuition, act with integrity, and build trust.

Communicate with Honesty

I used to take Jake's negative moods personally. I assumed I was the cause of them because he unintentionally took it out on me. And if his mood lasted a long time, I wondered if he still loved me or even liked me. Later I would find out that the root cause had nothing to do with me. He needed to open up and tell me what was going on instead of letting his bad mood get between us. With honest communication, I could have empathized instead of jumping to conclusions. It could have brought us together instead of tearing us further apart.

Also, disagreements happen and it's okay. Sometimes our emotions get out of control and we get carried away in the moment. Talking about a situation after things have cooled off can be beneficial for understanding each other, preventing it from happening again, or knowing how to handle it better next time. If something continues to nag at my conscience, it usually means I need to apologize and make amends.

Be honest and vulnerable, tell people what is going on, reflect, and apologize when necessary.

Draw the Line

There was a time when our marriage was close to falling apart. Jake was at his heaviest weight, drank a lot of alcohol, and worked long hours,

185

all of which was a trifecta for snoring loudly every night. I would try to roll him over or shake him awake, but then it would start again as soon as he drifted back to sleep.

I couldn't take it.

Lack of sleep makes me feel terrible, not to mention super grouchy, and it started adding up in a big way. After reaching my threshold for severe sleep deprivation, I finally told him we had to sleep in separate bedrooms. He was hurt and angry and huffed down to the guest bedroom. I didn't know how it was going to end.

I had to draw the line and advocate for my well-being. I stood strong, probably because I was so physically exhausted that I had no choice. It was the most painful moment of our marriage, and I knew it could permanently impact our relationship. But I had to risk it and I had to let go of the outcome.

Sleeping next to each other had been the only time we spent together. It was all we had left. Separating our bedrooms eliminated our only moments of connection. It could have caused a rift in our marriage too difficult to mend. It could have led to a bigger separation than just sleeping arrangements. Divorce was not out of the question. And it was much more than just snoring, it was Jake's negativity, depression, and absence. He was not the same person that I had married. Everything was on the line.

When you get to your breaking point in a relationship, declare your ultimatum and let go. Stand your ground and accept that it may not end with a happy reunion.

Trust Actions Over Words

We had reached a fork in the road. Jake knew that this was his moment to step up, or we would continue drifting apart. He was going to lose me, and this was the wake-up call that he needed. Jake's lifestyle choices had caused his snoring and the person he had become, and it was driving me away. He couldn't just *tell* me that he was going to fix it, he *had* to fix it. He knew that our future together hinged on his actions. So he did the work and turned it around.

He lost weight, cut back on drinking, prioritized a better sleep schedule, and stopped snoring. With his actions, he proved that I was important to him. Through all those years when he couldn't change his lifestyle and habits for his own benefit, he was finally able to do it to save our marriage.

Trust is important in every relationship. One of the things that bothers Jake the most is having faith in someone's word, and then being let down over and over again. He gets angry at himself when he offers his trust but then is repeatedly fooled or misled. And when the snoring issue came between us, I expected the same thing—action, not words.

Sometimes relationships are not meant to be, and separation is the best outcome for everyone involved. This is what happened with the family farm. We finally stepped up and gave an ultimatum. We could no longer accept the promises that the transition would work itself out, we needed action. And when the action never came, we had to let go.

It was a painful divorce from the family business. It resulted in a separation from our extended family, our careers, our community, our home, and our identities all at the same time. And yet, the pain of the separation was the only way forward for everyone involved.

If there are challenges that come up in your relationships, trust action and behavior over words. Sadly, we see a lot of couples who are at this point in their marriage. It's time for one of them to finally demand some action instead of listening to excuses or empty promises over and over again.

Bouncing Back

After we hit "below rock bottom" and slowly climbed our way back out again, I started seeing the real Jake show through little by little. It was the Jake that I remembered from high school. He was regaining his confident, fun, free-thinking, rebellious spirit. I could barely contain my excitement. But it was only short glimpses, and it was devastating when he regressed. Sometimes having my hopes dashed down was almost more painful than having hope at all.

Slowly, ever so slowly, his spirit regained its strength. It would show up for longer periods of time and return more often. Then it dawned on me, *Oh my God, our kids are finally going to meet the real Jake! They could have the dad that they were always meant to have.* That thought has inspired me to stay the course and stay strong during my times of doubt.

Not only did Jake pull through to meet the standards of his past high school self, but he has surpassed them by far. Jake is now healthier physically, mentally, emotionally, and spiritually, and his energy has recaptured that magnetic attraction that first drew me to him. And I know he feels the same about me.

I love to imagine having a conversation with my seventeen-year-old self, that high school junior with low self-esteem. I would walk into that band room, look her in the eyes, and tell her to keep working, keep improving, and never never *never* stop growing. All of the hard work is worth it! I imagine telling her who she will marry and about the life they will build together. Even my cool high school senior self would be speechless and ecstatic.

Today our marriage is stronger than ever before thanks to all the lessons we learned in this chapter. We inspire each other to grow and elevate more every day. But we aren't perfect, and we are never done. We encounter new and different challenges within our relationship. We continue to learn new ways to navigate through them.

When people grow together, their individual potential is exponentially increased. But when relationships start to pull apart, they can create a burden that seems too much to bear. It's impossible to grow at the same rate all the time, but you both must keep growing and supporting each other's unique path of personal development. Everyone needs motivation in different ways, so cautiously navigate each relationship to find the best methods and outcomes.

If your partner is in a low spot, you may be called to be the strong one for a while. Maybe a long while. Don't join them in their depression, inspire them to take action and rise above it. Their true being is hiding underneath the darkness, needing your light to guide them.

Own your side of the relationship by controlling yourself, caring for yourself, rising up to your full potential, and increasing your own attraction. Support them by encouraging their independence, complimenting everything good, setting a good example, and holding space. Power up your relationship by serving unconditionally, aligning your goals, leaning into your unique strengths, and prioritizing growth as a team. Unite with integrity by communicating honestly, drawing the line when necessary, and building trust with actions over words.

If you are staring at someone from across the room, then rise up to meet them at their exciting new level. No one and nothing is out of reach. If they don't see you today, then keep working until they do. If you were lucky enough to marry that person, never settle down. Never settle. Never go backward.

Always keep growing and elevating together.

CHAPTER 10

Never Stop Growing

Jake joked that I wouldn't return to Minnesota after my yoga retreat in Costa Rica.

I couldn't help but smile at him. I joked back, saying, "No, I'll come back and get you and the kids. I won't leave you behind." The words effortlessly tumbled out without really thinking about them. We didn't take it seriously at the time, but we should have. There was something deep down that was pulling both of us to Costa Rica.

Less than two years later, that playful conversation has come true. Jake was right—part of me stayed in Costa Rica. I never fully returned to Minnesota. And I was right too—I came back to get him and the kids. We did not realize it then, but our relocation had begun.

Throughout the process of writing this book, our lives have dramatically changed. Jake and I, along with our twelve-year-old daughter, Avery, and our ten-year-old daughter, Maya, visited Costa Rica a few times. We traveled around the diverse country and found our dream home—a brand-new condo in the hills of Central Valley.

In August of 2024, we packed a twenty-foot shipping container with our furniture and belongings and sent it across the ocean. We spent a couple more months in Minnesota living out of suitcases, getting rid of all the things we couldn't bring with us, and wrapping up our lives there. In October, we said goodbye to our family and friends, then flew to Costa Rica with an extra seat for Maya's cello.

Our new-construction condo wasn't quite finished, so we continued living out of suitcases in a temporary unit, getting our kids acclimated to a new culture, and learning Spanish. We flew back to Minnesota to celebrate Christmas, then returned to Costa Rica with our cat, Partner, and our family unit was reunited once again.

In January of 2025, we moved into our new condo, unloaded all our beloved belongings from the shipping container, and we have been finding our new normal ever since.

While I had the pleasure of writing this book, Jake took on all the logistical responsibilities of the relocation, which took more time, energy, dedication, and patience than we ever expected. Moving to Costa Rica wasn't just about letting go of our past; it was also about proving our commitment to the future. It has been more challenging and more rewarding than we could have ever imagined.

Today we breathe the air, drink the water, and love the beautiful climate that surrounds us all year long. We live in a three-bedroom condo with tall ceilings and a fraction of the "stuff" we had just a few years ago. Our deck overlooks the stunning landscape, and we open our wall of patio doors to blur the boundaries of inside and outside. We go to the farmer's market every week to buy fresh fruit, vegetables, meat, eggs, honey, and coffee. Our circadian rhythm syncs up with the year-round, twelve-hour daylight cycle. We have time for ourselves, for each other, and to connect with nature.

We live among a community of new friends from all over the world. Our daughters attend a bilingual school, participate in a local orchestra, and love swimming in our condominium's pool. Jake and I are dedicating our lives to helping others find joy, love, health, and purpose. At the same time, we continue to find more layers to our own joy, love, health, and purpose. We have found our paradise.

But paradise does not come without its challenges. In fact, it would be boring and repetitive if it didn't. There are rainy seasons, dry seasons, and active volcanoes. There are cultural differences, language barriers, and we struggle to fit in. We encounter difficult feelings, bad moods, and disagreements. We get overwhelmed and have self-doubt. We encounter stress and anxiety. But working through all of this is part of the journey and part of our growth. Every day is a new adventure.

I thought I would feel different the moment we moved to Costa Rica. I thought I would be a completely new person. But moving to Costa Rica did not change us.

It was the journey leading up to the move that changed us.

We spent years evolving into the people we are today and then realized that those people no longer fit the farm life in Minnesota. Our inner world changed first, then the outer world followed. We didn't create the destination; we opened our true selves to discover it.

This Is Not The End

If you feel stuck in life, we have amazing news: this is not the end.

What if I don't like my job or my life??? **This is not the end.**

What if I feel depressed, unhealthy, and overweight??? **This is not the end.**

What if I hate the person I see in the mirror??? **This is not the end.**

The scariest part of feeling stuck is that you believe it is permanent and your trajectory is irreversible.

But this is not the end.

You can change, and you must open your mind to see the options. In fact, life around you will continue to evolve, and everything will change with or without your permission. It will be much more painful if you try to stay put.

When we broke the news to our family and friends that we were moving to Costa Rica, one of the biggest questions we were asked was, "Are you moving there *permanently*?!"

We would answer gently, "Well, no, nothing is permanent. But we are moving there with all of our belongings. We plan to live there full-time. We'll try it for a few years. Then, who knows? We might choose to live somewhere else in the future. This doesn't have to be forever."

Freedom!

Freedom from feeling stuck. Freedom from feeling like every decision has to be permanent. Freedom from the belief that our lives are set in stone. Freedom from the expectations of others. Freedom from our misleading limiting beliefs. Freedom to grow and change every day. We are finally free to be Generation Zero.

We know that this is not the end. Our lives will continue to change and evolve. It is our job to guide ourselves in the right direction with our daily habits, thought patterns, beliefs, behavior, and mindset. We will continue revisiting, refining, strengthening, and building on the six phases of our Brilliant Life Journey. Above all, we will prioritize learning and growing.

This may be the last chapter of the book, but it certainly is not the end. I hope that in ten years, we will be amazed at how much more we have grown and how much farther we have traveled.

Each day, I try to hear the wisdom of my future self. What advice is that person giving me right now so that I can continue growing? What is she trying to tell me?

> *Live with no regrets.*
> *Fulfill your soul's purpose.*
> *Make the world a better place.*

Looking back, what do I need to tell my past self from ten years ago? What advice does she need to hear from me?

> *Follow the white rabbit.*
> *Take the red pill.*
> *Anything is possible.*

But what does that mean exactly?

> *Rock bottom is your wake-up call—use the pain to take action.*
> *Listen to the warning signs, tune in to your intuition, and question the path ahead of you.*
> *Find your edge, declare an ultimatum, and then courageously let go.*
> *Contemplate with inner reflection and self-awareness.*
> *Investigate your unique sources of joy and purpose.*
> *Activate your physical, mental, emotional, and spiritual health.*
> *Eliminate everything holding you back.*

Accelerate your personal development, challenge yourself, and step into your new reality.
Navigate your relationships and grow exponentially together.

I started writing this book to help you, but I think I had to write this book for myself. It was to heal the wounds of my past, to remind myself of all the lessons I have learned, to teach myself how to live a more brilliant life, and to appreciate the journey. This book has been a way for me to talk to myself and finally listen. I can't ignore the written words like I have ignored the verbal ones. This book is a love letter to my past, present, and future self. And to yours.

The Ultimate Goal is Self-Love

Each of the Six Phases, all of the Focus Areas within them, and every single one of the Action Steps are aimed at one massive, final goal: finding self-love.

We did not realize it at the time, but everything we have learned and worked toward over the past decade has been a journey toward self-love. We started below rock bottom and slowly built from the ground up. It was a slow, steady process, but the results were miraculous. We finally believe in ourselves and our dreams.

Cultivating self-love is our goal for you.

We want you to find as much self-love as you possibly can so that you have the confidence to take action toward your goals. So you have the self-respect to follow your intuition and values. So you have the desire to take care of your body and mind in the healthiest way. So you feel worthy of pursuing the life of your dreams. So you stop holding yourself back and find your own paradise.

So you realize that you can do anything.

Every thought you have, every action you take, and every daily habit you create will impact your life. The smallest things add up to massive changes. If you truly want to change your life, you have to start making those small changes. Just a little bit of movement means that you are no longer stuck. You can reinvent yourself. You can reinvent your life.

Take one small step. Then another.

Find the white rabbit, and don't let it out of your sight.

The choice is now yours . . . and the red pill is waiting for you.

Connect with Us

Visit our website brilliantlifejourney.com
Follow us on YouTube and social media @BrilliantLifeJourney
Podcast: *A More Brilliant Life: Stories of Reinvention*
You can also follow our family on YouTube @CostaRicaGenZero

Acknowledgements

To our daughter, Avery: Thank you for bringing joy and energy into our lives. You teach us to laugh, act silly, and appreciate all the details.

To our daughter, Maya: Thank you for bringing love and light into our lives. You teach us to slow down, cuddle, and appreciate the still moments together.

To my mom, Lorie: Thank you for gifting me the pursuit of adventure and a defiant spirit to step outside the box. You inspire me to be strong.

In honor of my dad, Garry, who always believed in me. I saw it in his eyes, heard it in his words, and today I feel it coursing through my veins.

To Jake's mom, Janet: Thank you for being the most selfless and generous caregiver. You have a bigger heart than anyone we know.

To Jake's dad, Dave: Thank you for bringing your good energy to every situation. It solves more problems than you realize.

To all our siblings: Thanks for always having our back. We know we can call on you for absolutely anything. You are the foundation of our support system.

To our life coach, Julie: You are our hero. You came into our lives at the perfect moment and guided us out of an impossible mess.

To all of our coaches, mentors, and instructors: Your knowledge, advice, and support has been a pivotal part of our transformation.

To our yoga retreat hosts and healers, especially Julie, Tacy, and Rachel: Thank you for changing our lives and changing the world. We would not be here today without the wellness experiences and spiritual guidance that you offer.

To everyone at StoryBuilders, especially Jen, Tracy, Jesse, and Bill: You are amazing at what you do. Thank you for your expertise, patience, flexibility, support, and for making this dream a reality.

To all of our friends back in Minnesota: Thank you for helping us through a very difficult time in our lives. Your laughter and love got us through to the other side. We miss you.

To all of our new friends in Costa Rica: The warm welcome and your immediate, unconditional friendship has made all the difference. We feel at home with you.

To the generations who came before us and paved the way: We are honored to continue the legacy that your spirits pioneered.

To everyone who played a part in our midlife crisis, midlife awakening and dramatic personal transformation: You will always be a part of our story. Thank you.

Endnotes

1 Akira the Don, Jordan B Peterson's Drinking Song (Meaning-wave, 2019).
2 ibid
3 ibid

About the Authors

Kylie and Jake Rieke are certified life coaches, writers, podcast hosts, entrepreneurs, personal growth advocates, health & fitness enthusiasts, and proud parents of two dynamic daughters.

Kylie is a Registered Yoga Teacher (RYT) 200, certified meditation teacher, Reiki master and has a degree in studio art.

Jake is certified in civil, divorce & family mediation, has a degree in psychology and sociology, and completed the MARL two-year leadership program.

Kylie and Jake have been married for over twenty years, serving two of those years in the United States Peace Corps El Salvador.

After an epic mid-life crisis, they flipped their lives from laboring on a farm in Minnesota to living their dream life in Costa Rica. They went from obesity, pre-diabetes, and asthma to completing a marathon, a Tough Mudder, and a Spartan race within a single year. Together, they developed the six phases of the Brilliant Life Journey method to help others take ownership and action toward a healthier and more meaningful life.